A prominent and well  startling sequence of ev landed on her property occurs close by a Roya shelter. So alarmed are t their Member of Parlia munications and inciden ...ows, resulting in a personal visit by a very high ranking RAF officer. He gives his own opinion on the phenomena, but entreats the witnesses to keep the whole affair secret.

But follow-up inquiries suggest that some of the information involved is so delicate that not even Parliament is being told the truth. Here are the facts, revealed for the first time in startling and bold authenticity.

Peter Paget

The Welsh Triangle

PANTHER
GRANADA PUBLISHING
London Toronto Sydney New York

Published by Granada Publishing Limited
in Panther Books 1979

ISBN 0 586 04911 8

A Panther UK Original
Copyright © Peter Paget 1979

Granada Publishing Limited
Frogmore, St Albans, Herts AL2 2NF
and
3 Upper James Street, London W1R 4BP
866 United Nations Plaza, New York, NY10017, USA
117 York Street, Sydney, NSW 2000, Australia
100 Skyway Avenue, Rexdale, Ontario, M9W 3A6, Canada
PO Box 84165, Greenside, 2034 Johannesburg, South Africa
CML Centre, Queen & Wyndham, Auckland 1, New Zealand

Set, printed and bound in Great Britain by
Cox & Wyman Ltd, Reading
Set in Monotype Times

This book is dedicated to my wife Jane, without whose endless help and encouragement its production would have been impossible.

Acknowledgments

The presentation of this book would not have been possible without the kind assistance of over 3,000 people, sincere and intelligent citizens, who have written to me during the last two years reporting their sightings and experiences. I would like to thank those families in the West Wales area who have given so freely and generously of their time and hospitality in the course of the research that has resulted in this book: in particular, Billy and Pauline Coombs and their family; Rose and Hayden Granville of the Haven Fort Hotel; and the residents of the villages of Little Haven and Broad Haven and the good townspeople of Haverfordwest and Milford Haven.

I am grateful especially to my friend and colleague Professor Hans Holzer, of New York, for his ceaseless enthusiasm and his contribution towards our work; and special thanks go to Commander H. Penrose, Mrs D. Mills and my fellow researchers into this, the world's most baffling mystery.

Sincere gratitude also to Pauline Penn and my wife Jane for secretarial, editorial and research assistance.

Contents

Introduction

Sleepy Welsh villages, rolling golden sands set against the stark, jagged Pembrokeshire coastline. A scene of beautiful tranquillity, overlooking the Atlantic Ocean and St Brides Bay, littered with rocks and islands; a haven for coastal shipping in times of storm.

Isolated, unspoilt, untouched and remote! The sort of place where you take your kids on holiday. Hardly the setting for a most startling series of events which occurred during 1977 and 1978 and, indeed, continue to this day. For here in the quiet Welsh countryside took place a scenario involving aliens from outer space, the British and American governments, possibly even the Russians.

For those of us who have studied UFOs, a term that superseded the original 'Flying Saucers' of Kenneth Arnold fame in 1947, the UFO trail is a long, arduous and highly frustrating one. What we know has always been dwarfed by the magnitude of the questions left unanswered. It would seem that thirty years or more of research, diligent collating of every known fact and intensive investigation have left us with precious little for our efforts. Everyone is waiting for a breakthrough.

When I first came to hear of the story that I am about to relate, I was Editor of one of the leading UFO magazines. I was familiar with the majority of events, reported daily in different parts of the world, of inexplicable sightings of aerial craft, even landings and reports of strange people seen emerging from them. Information flowed in from press-cutting services, from more than fifty specialist magazines published all over the western world and from personal contacts with researchers in other countries.

Strangely, it was with almost complete disregard that I

first noticed the occasional report coming from areas of the Welsh coastline: such sightings as, 'red, green and white lights, reported by coastguards, over the Bristol Channel'. I dismissed them! They were too easy to explain. Every aircraft carries these colours. They were obviously a misidentification.

However, more reports confronted the British public: 'Terror Triangle', heralded the *Sun*; 'Giant Spacemen', the *Western Mail*; 'UFOs Galore', the *Daily Express* – this smoke could not possibly be substantiated on anything less than some fire.

Had the 'silly season' broken out in rural Wales? Was Fleet Street hard pushed for a news story? Obviously not, for reports were coming in from schoolteachers, indeed whole classes of schoolchildren numbering fourteen or more; doctors, firemen, police – people who are trained observers were seeing the identical phenomena sighted by ordinary people. Something was obviously going on and, amazingly, nobody seemed the slightest bit interested.

Or were they?

My first trip to Wales revealed little more than I already knew by reading the newspapers. I spoke to the schoolchildren at Broad Haven Primary School, every one of them. Yes, all this was as reported in the *Observer* Colour Supplement: I saw the pictures the children had drawn independently of each other, showing the same silver, circular landed craft, with two individuals coming from it and examining the local sewerage facility which lay just a field away from the school.

Could fourteen independent minds between the ages of nine and eleven years old, without commercial incentive, and uncluttered by the psychological stress common in our society, produce such uniformity of account? Highly unlikely. Could they have seen a helicopter and mistaken it for some spacecraft, for they were certain that this is what it was? Such trivial thoughts were quickly dismissed by a minor argument between two of the children as to whether

10

my car was a Lotus Europa or an Esprit. Having correctly settled between them that it was a Europa, they had succeeded in convincing me that their precision of observation left no room for the possibility of the sighted object having been a helicopter. Indeed these kids would probably have known the make and country of origin of any aircraft.

Their teacher, Mrs Morgan, a homely and friendly woman, was a little reluctant at first but later helpful in her approach to what had happened. I sensed that here lay perhaps a little more than shyness or embarrassment. For I was aware that, in the press, only the children had been reported as having seen the object. She led me to one side. 'I saw it too, you know,' she said. 'It was real.'

Her eyes questioned my reaction, expecting a rebuff. 'Of course it was,' I said reassuringly. She smiled, her anxiety turned into relief. At least somebody believed her. She went on, 'You know, when they went, a little whirlwind of dust came across the playground.' She paused. 'It was almost as if they were saying goodbye.'

I felt moved. There was something about the way she related the story, a simple sighting which I had read from many parts of the world many times before, which made very clear to me that her experience had touched her deeply, had given her some kind of profound realization. It was, perhaps, the kind of thing so many of us spend half our lives searching for: the unquestionable certainty that somewhere, we don't know where, there is somebody else, something else – out there!

Travelling on and meeting other people with comparable experiences, it was obvious that sighting a UFO affected all of the witnesses differently. It struck in some witnesses a chord, something almost intangible, not easy to relate, something beyond the normal run of human experience. Indeed the difficulty to relate what had happened was one of the most consistent characteristics one noticed about the reports; that, together with a shy reluctance to admit all that they knew, I sensed that relatives and friends had not

11

been too kind, and the usual jest of having one too many at the local was bandied about freely. It is obviously not easy when people closest to you question your state of mind, or maybe it was just that they did not want to admit that they themselves might have seen something.

I find that people are always searching for normality – to be included, never excluded, from that which is considered the norm; to be accepted. So how difficult it is for people who have been involved in events that, within any frame of reference, seem totally unacceptable.

The unacceptability became more intense as I investigated even deeper: beyond 'The Welsh Triangle' – as the press had clichéd it.

Broad Haven, Pembrokeshire   P.P.
May 1978

The only question that remains is, where do they come from?

Astronaut Edward Mitchell, commenting on UFOs

1

'UFOs Galore'

It was Thursday, 11 August 1977. Jane hurried into the bedroom.

'It's Professor Hans Holzer on the telephone from America.'

I put aside my notes and walked swiftly down the hall to the small untidy office, that seemed to overflow with books and piles of papers. The walls were covered with charts and pictures showing fuzzy outlines, lights in the sky, dark disc-shaped objects and detailed close-ups of burnt undergrowth and circular depressions. I squeezed behind the desk and lifted the receiver.

'Hello, Hans. Where are you, New York?'

Hans's voice came faintly over the line, instantly recognizable by his middle European accent. He sounded frustrated and tired. 'I've had terrible trouble with the airlines. We can't get into London, everyone's on strike. I've tried everyone – Lufthansa, British Airways, Pan-Am. We can't even come in via Paris! I'm in Los Angeles with the film crew. We will just have to come later in the year. Go to Wales and see all the witnesses and explain to them that we do need them, but later on. Explain that it's completely out of our control. There's nothing I can do,' Hans ended abruptly.

'Sure,' I replied. 'I'll have to go down, as everything is arranged. Some of the people aren't on the phone and there is no way I can cancel the interviews.'

Hans's voice came again, 'Don't worry, go down and tell them it's all right, we will be there later. But there is no way I can get round this problem, Heathrow is in chaos.'

We chatted on, sorting out a few technicalities. I was disappointed, but all was not lost. Hans had worked so hard

15

to try and produce *The Ufonauts**, a factual documentary on UFOs and everything seemed to have stood in its way. Now of all infuriating things a strike at London Airport had completely cut off our transportation. All the interviews that we had arranged with the witnesses of the events that had happened in West Wales would have to be re-run. I did not look forward to the job of going down and making our apologies, but it was my responsibility and at least it would allow me to familiarize myself with the situation. For twelve months now we had been collecting information for the film from all over the world. Of all the areas that had proved especially intriguing, the reports from the Pembrokeshire coast had been the most detailed.

I returned to the bedroom, but my mind was too active for sleep. So, picking up the large grey file marked 'UFOs – unexplained cases', I settled into bed and thumbed through the voluminous file.

My interest in the Welsh reports had been aroused in early February when newspapers told of a sighting by a Mrs Louise Bassett. Louise and her husband, both aged thirty-one, run a gourmet restaurant in Carmarthen and have a delightful house set in six wooded acres in Ferryside. David is a crack shot, a first-class angler and an international power-boat racer. Their credibility was unquestionable and they certainly were not the sort of people to be making flippant or hysterical reports of UFOs, or to carry out any kind of hoax.

It is a ten-mile journey from their Carmarthen restaurant to their home and Louise was driving back in the early hours through the darkened Welsh countryside. The air was heavy with thunder and low-lying cloud obscured the stars. It was with some degree of alarm that she described her sighting:

'At Idole I saw in the fields on the far right a brown mass with flat blue lights intermittently flashing. My first reaction was that there had been an accident farther up the road.

*A film based on the book *The Ufonauts*, by Hans Holzer, now published in the UK by Panther Books.

16

'The thing looked as if it was hovering in the air. My car radio went completely on the blink and there was tremendous interference.'

Louise travelled on towards Towy Castle, then she saw the lights moving towards Trimsaran.

'When I reached the spot where I thought it had been, there was nothing. I've never seen anything like it before. I've got 20/20 vision and I was 100 per cent sober. I've never believed in this sort of thing before.'

Completely mystified by her experience, Mrs Bassett made some inquiries but could find no rational explanation.

'The police told me that no police cars, fire appliances or ambulances had been anywhere near that spot.'

Apparently neither RAF nor private helicopters were operating.

The radio interference had been very widespread and at the same time that Louise's radio blew, people all over the area were making complaints to radio dealers, the BBC and the ITA about signal strength throughout that night. It had fallen off so badly that colour sets reverted to black and white. However, the BBC was certain that there had been no reduction in transmitted signal.

It was in almost exactly the same location one month later that more Carmarthenshire residents witnessed a similar happening, again in the early hours.

John Petts is a prominent Welsh artist particularly noted for his designs of stained-glass windows. Like many creative people he often works at unconventional hours to finish a particular commission. One night he was in at his home, which enjoys a magnificent view across the estuary. He described the following strange occurrence:

'It was just after 1.00 a.m. and I was preparing for bed after drinking some black coffee. I had been working late as I often do and I had switched off the lights in the living-room. I drew back the curtains and looked south-eastwards across the estuary above and beyond the horizon of hills overlooking Ferryside on the far side of the river.

17

'My eye was caught by a horizontal strip of light, a luminous pale gold like the colour of the moon. In fact, I said to myself: That must be part of the moon showing through a gap in the clouds. By now, understandably, I was looking intently indeed. I must add that I have specially good far sight and by profession I am a visually objective observer and recorder.

'I was amazed to see that the outline shape of light was clear and sharp, far from woolly edged as it would be from a cloud. What I saw clearly was a clean-cut shape of even light, pale gold, the shape of a weaver's shuttle; sharply pointed at each end, the top and bottom edges straight and parallel.

'By now I was intent and alert wondering what will this do, for it was poised and immobile. I thought: Will it rise higher or will it move to the right or left? In fact, it did not move at all, but suddenly it was switched off, just like switching off a light.'

Mrs Teasey, a neighbour of Mr Petts, also saw the phenomenon at 1.10 a.m.; while another Llanstephan woman, Mrs Michael Lownes, the wife of an agricultural engineer, said: 'Mr Petts's description put into words what I saw around last Christmas. I walked from my sitting-room, looked through the window and stopped in my tracks. Above the level of the land was an extraordinary bright light where there was no reason for a light to be. I am not the sort of person who would believe in UFOs. My inclination is to say "Rubbish", but this I *did* see.'

Reports of unidentified flying objects were not uncommon from Wales. Shortly before Louise Bassett sighted her UFO, a fifty-nine-year-old Aberavon man, Mr Arthur Sugg of Sandown Road, a retired steelworks roller-man, had reported the following: 'I was out walking on Aberavon sea-front with my Airedale, Tuscan. It was shortly before noon and I was at the Briton Ferry end of the promenade. The cloud was very low. It was not raining but it was misty. I was looking out towards Mumbles headland when there was a break in the clouds. It was then that I saw what I can only describe as a dome-shaped object. It was moving in a northerly direction. I watched it for between five and ten seconds until the gap in the clouds closed.'

In January and February of the same year, John Ridge, a freelance photographer of Carmarthen, had observed low-flying lights but with no sound at all. They were flying northwest over Wauniago, Carmarthen at 9.00 one evening. Also in January, from Carmarthen, he had witnessed at sunset the passage of an object estimated to be the size of a Boeing 707 which had a glowing head and three divergent trails, unlike either con-trails or a comet.

Previously, on 19 November 1976 at 5.20 p.m., a sixteen-year-old youth, Brian Jones, of Llanerch, Llanelli, Dyfed had observed a very bright white light moving slowly above his district.

'It varied in brightness as it moved. I realized that what I was looking at was definitely not an aeroplane, a helicopter, or any other aircraft, because it travelled low and made no noise. I began to get so excited about the object that I ran to my house, and as I came to our side entrance I looked up behind my shoulder and there, closer to where I was standing, I saw that the light had brightened to a yellowish, round fireball with, underneath, a bright emission of sparks. As I was excited and a little bit frightened about it, I ran in at our backdoor and told my mother about the light, for her to see it. But when she came outside, it had completely disappeared.'

At that time, Jupiter was visible in the eastern sky and Venus was very low in the western sky; and apparently the UFO had given the impression that there were two objects in the sky at the same time, of the same magnitude as Venus. Brian, something of a student of astronomy, was certain it was not any natural phenomena. Indeed he had been witness to a much closer encounter in 1973. This also had occurred in the month of November and it took the form of a low-flying cigar-shaped object. It was yellow in colour at

19

both ends and emitting some kind of fluorescent glow, with a bright red light in the middle. The object had hovered at a distance of no more than 250 metres from the witness, directly over the supermarket in his local town. So vivid was his impression of the UFO that he had supplied me with a detailed drawing.

Before the sightings that were now being reported from the extreme western corner of Wales, Snowdonia seemed to have been particularly favoured as an area rich in graphic reports. Two sightings had been made by the same person, separated by only forty-eight hours, on 28 and 30 June 1976. The observer, Brian Guiver, of Wallington, Surrey was on holiday and was driving down the A4086 from Llanrug to Cym-y-glo, towards the south-east: 'We had Mount Snowdon in view. It was while looking at Snowdon that I spotted a large black object in the sky. It was moving towards the peak of Snowdon, from the mountain to the left of Snowdon's peak. I said, "What's that?" I saw it for about ten seconds, before a hill on the right blocked it from sight.'

He further stated: 'Two days later, whilst I was climbing Snowdon and looking at birds in the sky, and anything else, after the first sighting, I suddenly saw three objects flying in formation at about 2,000 feet. They were zigzagging all over the place, but still keeping in formation all the time at quite a speed. When the sunlight hit one of the objects as it turned, I could see the bottom of it and the outside was silver and the inside a primrose colour. It was just like a saucer in shape. After keeping watch for about ten seconds or so, I took a photograph of them in the distance but it did not come out.'

I can sympathize with Brian Guiver's problem in trying to obtain a photograph, for with a conventional lens a high-flying object at considerable range is almost indiscernible on a negative, the 'dot' even becoming blurred into obscurity if it is moving at high speed. As most popular cameras rarely operate at faster than 1/90th of a second, their chances of capturing or 'freezing' moving objects are very slim.

One of the few successful pictures of a UFO was taken by Gordon Hipperson, a professional photographer, and this was only achieved in brilliant sunlight, with a tripod-mounted camera, at an exposure time of 1/500th of a second at f16, using 800 ASA Tri-X film. Even under these ideal conditions the photograph, showing an elliptical, saucer-shaped object, was still blurred, which indicated that the object's speed could have been in excess of 4,000 mph.

Jane, my lifelong partner on the trail of the UFOs, has also described a spectacular sighting which took place in the early 1970s while she was staying at a cottage 2,000 feet up in the Snowdonia mountains:

'It was a brilliant, sunny day with blue sky and perfect "mountain-air" visibility. I was looking out over the lake that fills the bottom of the valley when suddenly this huge, very heavy looking, metallic "cigar" flew quietly down the valley at the same height above the lake as my cottage; hence I was looking at it directly from one side, with the steepness of the mountain drop below me. The sunlight glinted off its aluminium-like surface and it was clearly no airship, for it had no aerofoils or markings on its surface of any kind. It was perfectly smooth, just like polished metal, not shiny like chromium but that kind of dull-bright aluminium you get these days. It passed by me at no greater distance than 300 metres and was travelling quite slowly. It was absolutely silent. To my amazement, when it reached a junction of the valleys over the end of the lake, it stopped and turned on its central axis, ninety degrees and moved off out of my sight towards the slate quarries. I ran around the mountain to try and get another view of it, but it had passed from my sight beyond the towering peaks. It was a very beautiful thing; it seemed tremendously powerful, and yet sublime. When you have seen something like that, it's very difficult to describe; the feeling you get is like nothing else.'

A classic 'close encounter of the first kind'.

Throughout 1977 reports continued to arrive almost by

the week. The latest one was dated 1 August and appeared under the headline, 'Mountain UFO Mystery'.

It appeared that an unidentified flying object had been seen above Betws mountain by two people on their way to work: Mrs Janet Box of Glanamman, and Mr Grevette of Salem, Llandeilo. The object, which resembled a large silver football, was seen crossing the mountain and flashing in the sunlight at 7.40 a.m. Mrs Box said that it hovered like a helicopter in one place and that it was brilliant silver. Mr Grevette said that 'it wasn't a plane and was definitely not a bird'.

The possibility of its being a meteorological balloon was denied, and the Flight Lieutenant Duty Officer with RAF Brawdy's operations wing said that it had been too low to be a weather balloon.

This last sighting was similar to one which had been described by Mrs S. Birchall of Llysfaen. She had noticed an unusual aerial object at midnight, one clear July night.

She related: 'I live in a particularly elevated spot, and when putting the dog out just after midnight, I could not fail to see a large star-like object shining brilliantly golden amid the weak greenish light of the stars. It was about two-thirds of the distance between Betws-yn-Rhos and Rhyd-y-Foel; nearer the latter. Observed through binoculars it seemed to be turning as it varied between what looked like a clockface, an ellipse, and then a completely sideways view of a circle. It faced towards the sea all the time and seemed to have a projection like a nose in the centre of the circle; and behind were flames spreading out like hair. These were reddish, but the front part was a very bright orange yellow, with several dark marks resembling square windows. The aeroform was rough looking, not smooth, and seen without the aid of binoculars it was as if it had a tail at the base. It was much bigger and brighter than the stars around. It was a clear night, no moon, but plenty of stars. Everything everywhere was very still and the object did not seem to be making much progress towards the sea, although it moved that way when viewed through the binoculars. It was so remarkable, to me!'

Another Welsh sighting had been made by Phil Vaughan and Llew Davies of Bridgend. They wrote to me: 'On Tuesday, 1 February 1977 at 07.57 hours three of us, all adults, watched for about seven minutes a long cigar-shaped object, low on the horizon in a southeast direction. As we watched, it moved across the skyline; twice it stopped for a while, then went out of sight. A few days later came the TV report about some children seeing something similar land near their school in West Wales.'

These reports were typical of many thousands of similar ones which had been sent in all over the world, but also from the West Wales area had come a recent spate of descriptions of more spectacular events which promised to contain much more meaningful information. It was in the people who had witnessed these things that we were primarily interested, and on the following day we were to set off to that remote corner of the British Isles to meet them personally . . .

The morning was bright and sunny as we drove across the Severn Bridge, skimming like a bird over the grey waters over a hundred feet below.

'Welcome to Cymbru' read the sign. It flashed by and the needle again edged its way up around the seventies. Mile after mile of carriageway passed by, it seemed much farther than we had imagined, and even the M4 which penetrates deep into the heart of Wales these days did not shorten the journey. Cardiff passed by without much ado, the ring road keeping us well clear of the central traffic, and forty miles farther on the depressing but somewhat surrealist landscape of the oil refineries at Port Talbot swept into view. It was indeed a strange scene: bare, darkened hills sweeping down to an industrial complex which reached from one horizon to another. The air tanged of petro-chemicals, and airborne effluent belched from a thousand chimneys competing with each other to darken the skies.

The motorway made its way above the level of the chaos, cutting a straight and determined path through the steel madness of twentieth-century civilization. As we hurried away over the far hills I thought to myself that it was ironic that our methods of transportation were so dependent on an industry which could ravish the countryside and create this terrain.

However, once you have crossed the river at Carmarthen some miles farther on, and left the motorway behind for the A40, the horizon becomes more welcoming, green and fertile. We headed towards Pembrokeshire, in the new county of Dyfed. The Prescelly mountains, so called although they are really gentle hills rising only to 1,700 feet, loomed on the horizon to our right. It was from here, many thousands of years ago, that the 'Blue Stones' of Stonehenge were brought. Why the ancients should have taken monoliths many hundreds of miles to the distant Salisbury Plain is still a mystery, along with any really deep understanding of the significance of their Stone Age engineering. What did seem strange was that UFO activity seems to be more prolific where these ancient structures are found. However, we were to learn that this was only part of the story.

Haverfordwest, our temporary HQ for this trip, came into sight unexpectedly and proved to be a quaint, bustling little market town set high on a hill and overlooking a picturesque river and an old castle. The staff of the Mariners Hotel welcomed us and we settled comfortably in our rooms for the evening. Dinner was excellent.

The following day, the sun beat down out of a hot clear sky. We picked our way out of Haverfordwest, following the signpost to the village of Broad Haven. A narrow secondary road took us through sharp undulating hills displaying typical Atlantic coastal countryside. Short stunted trees in hedgerows leaned at angles of forty-five degrees, every twig of their structure marking the prevailing westerly wind. Squat, solid Pembrokeshire farmhouses nestled on the very edge of the road, capped with blue slate roofs and either

24

brightly whitewashed or left as resolute grey stone, depending on the taste of the owners. We cleared the crest of a hill and found ourselves descending steeply towards a long, curving golden beach, with the shining waters of St Brides Bay and the Atlantic Ocean beyond.

Our inquiries brought us to a narrow cul-de-sac and the local primary school, an unexpectedly modern building of brick and pre-fabricated classrooms. As our car drew up, a dozen children ran excitedly towards us, some clad in swimsuits, others in jeans and T-shirts.

'I'm looking for Mrs Morgan,' I began.

'She's inside,' excitedly proclaimed one child.

Two or three parents appeared from waiting cars. Everyone was helpful and friendly and in a huddle we were escorted into the classroom. The teacher, Mrs Morgan, was a bright, homely woman in her mid thirties, quietly but smartly dressed. We exchanged courtesies and on my suggestion retired to the playground outside where the children had first sighted their UFO.

The view was wide and uncluttered, looking out over neatly cut playing fields and surrounding farmland. The school was situated in a gentle valley at the head of which was a line of trees, just below the horizon, and some indistinctly discernible buildings no more than 300 or 400 yards away. We seated ourselves on the grass while Mrs Morgan quietened the children who were hustling to be the first to tell the story. I carefully noted all their names, just for the record. They were: Tudor Jones, Shaun Garrison, David George, Martin Evans, David Ward, Michael George, Philip Rees, Paul Williams, Jeremy Passmore, Andrew Lewis, Michael Webb, David Davies, Andrew Evans, and Lesley Neohorn.

Carefully I took the story from different members of the group. On 4 February 1977 they had all been playing football where we were now seated. Suddenly and almost simultaneously all of them had become aware of a strange, dome-shaped object just over 200 yards away, on the other side of a few trees near the head of the valley. It had been clearly visible, being close to the ground and only partly obstructed by two trees, one each side of it. The children had seen it against the background of the fields beyond, and it was below the skyline. David Davies, an articulate eleven-year-old who had seen the silver object first, told me that it was 'as big as a coach'.

'We couldn't believe it at first,' stated his friend, Michael Webb. 'One of the boys ran down the hill to tell Sir, but he didn't believe it. I watched it for between three and five minutes. It had a flashing red light and I'm sure it was a spaceship. It definitely wasn't a helicopter.'

Their companions, David Ward and Shaun Garrison, also saw it, and David wrote a description afterwards: 'The ship was silvery . . . The people had sort of cameras.'

Paul Williams went on: 'We saw something come out of it. It had a helmet. We ran and told Sir and when we went back it wasn't there.'

Shaun Garrison remembered: 'It was flattish and had ten or eleven windows and a door with a runway leading from the door, and it was silver.'

Philip Rees recalled: 'Shaun and David came running in and said that there was something there. So me and some other boys went up to the top of the playing field. We saw something silver and disc-shaped. There seemed to be a door opening from the object. David Davies and Tudor Jones saw a figure, they said it was silver. The object had a dome on the top of it, with a light. It was a very dull day, but I did see something.'

Michael Webb, aged ten, said: 'Everyone is sure that they saw something. It seemed cigar-shaped with a large dome on the top. I was frightened when I saw it.'

The headmaster, Mr Llewhellin, had interviewed all the children separately and also collectively afterwards and then asked them to go away into different rooms and independently draw what they had seen.

He said: 'Their stories were the same and have remained

the same. At my age, I'm naturally sceptical, but I'm convinced that they saw something. I do not believe primary school children are capable of a sustained, sophisticated hoax. The thread which appears to run through their stories is that the object was a silvery-yellow cigar shape with a dome and possibly a light on top.'

Mrs Morgan showed me a scrapbook they now keep on UFOs which contains as its first item the fourteen detailed drawings that the children had produced on what they had seen. Allowing for the fact that all the children were between nine and eleven years old, the graphics were quite informative.

The object seemed to have made a vivid impression on all of the children which was expressed by Philip Rees: 'It stuck in my mind.'

Michael Webb's father, Tim Webb, is a Squadron Leader overseeing the advanced instruction of fighter pilots at RAF Brawdy's Tactical Weapons Unit.

'I believe him implicitly,' said the Squadron Leader. 'I've yet to see a UFO, but I think there has to be something supernatural or paranormal.'

When queried as to whether he was worried about the description and the conventional silver colour of the object, he replied, 'No. It's logical that visitors would use a matt silver finish.' Adding that it was not only better for heat absorption, but offered the best chance of escaping unnoticed.

Strangely astute comment I thought, for a man who apparently knew nothing about the subject. Why indeed should the visitors wish to be 'unnoticed'?

Guided by two of the boys, I visited the exact spot over which the craft had been seen. The hillside behind us was quite steep, very uneven and muddy and, I thought, inaccessible to anything but a tractor. We were in a smallish field hemmed in by high trees and traversed by a 450-volt sub-station power line supported on wooden poles. No helicopter pilot in his right mind would come down here, and access by a light aircraft could not possibly have avoided a complete disaster. One of the boys pointed out a particular power-line pole which, he stated, the UFO had at one point touched. He indicated where the cross-T-piece metal was bent, and indeed it was out of true on this side by about thirty degrees. A little to the left, a substantial branch on one of the trees was strangely discoloured, the leaves being more yellow than on the rest of the trees.

'Most of the other children won't come here any more,' stated my guide, 'as they say it's haunted now.' (I noted that this implied that he was braver than the rest.)

A short distance away to our right, farther up the valley, was a small sewage-processing plant with a few filter-beds and outbuildings. There was certainly nothing here that could have given rise to a mis-identification. Back at the school all of the parents believed in the children's stories. Indeed there was the suggestion that one or two of them might have seen something themselves, although nothing specific was said. It did seem that some kind of aerial phenomenon had taken place at nearly the same location three days after the children had sighted theirs. Also, their teacher Mrs Morgan confided that she too had glimpsed the strange intruder.

She pointed to a brightly painted red, white and blue 'rocket'-like object set up beside the school's climbing frame. 'Our own UFO,' she said with amusement, going on to explain that when the story had broken in the press the children had arrived one morning to find this strange contraption dumped in their school yard. I recognized it as the empty wing tank of a jet fighter. Turning the practical joke to good advantage, the children had mounted the finned projectile and now it proudly adorned the school courtyard.

Time was pressing now, so with promises of a return visit we left our little group still discussing the origin of their UFO, and squeezed our way through the narrow streets towards Little Haven on the road to Dale, to interview more key witnesses.

An ordnance survey map is essential in this part of the

28

world for many of the signposts have either been defaced or completely removed, I gather by the Welsh Language Society, wherever the name does not comply with its Welsh counterpart; but being well versed in this problem throughout Cymru we threaded our way through the lanes banked with high grassy hedges. Coming down a long straight road by an old airfield, long disused, and ploughed up, we came to Ripperston Farm.

Pauline Coombs ushered us into the sitting-room. The farmhouse was pleasantly cool after the warmth of the car journey. The house was typical of Welsh farmhouses, with a huge kitchen and small gable-windowed bedrooms upstairs. Pauline settled us into armchairs and offered us tea. The story was long, complicated, and told with some reluctance at first. The Coombs family had had its fair share of visits by the press. It was good of them, I thought, to give up their time, and interviews had to be limited to those made by appointment over the telephone, due to the numbers of people interested in the happenings.

The Coombs family had first become involved in the strange scenario of events on the evening of 12 April 1977. Pauline had been driving the family's F-registered Hillman Hunter from St Ishmael's, accompanied by Kieron, her twelve-year-old son and her eight-year-old twin daughters Joanne and Layanne. They were travelling on the road over which Jane and I had just come, and were about a mile away from home on a straight narrow section bordered by wide verges, when suddenly Kieron had seen a light in the sky in front of them.

Pauline recalled: 'It was getting closer and it looked as though it would come through the windscreen. The thing went over us and the boy looked out of the back window to see if it kept on going.'

The object was no bigger than a football, yellowish in colour and had a torch-like beam spreading out from its underside towards the ground.

Kieron yelled that it had done a U-turn and was coming

alongside them now, on a parallel course. Pauline, unable to change direction on the long straight road, with neither turn-off nor opening, accelerated to eighty miles per hour – about the car's maximum – and floorboarded the car between the tunnel of high hedges on either side of the road.

The children, who were travelling in the rear seat, started to cry. Pauline, the car's headlights blazing, tore over the narrow humpbacked bridge praying that nothing was coming the other way. Stones and gravel flew as the car left the tarmac and slewed sideways down the farmtrack to her home, the UFO maintaining station a few feet away, just above the hedgerows.

The car bounced down the uneven track but, suddenly, in the evening gloom, the headlights faded, the engine cut out, and the car became a rolling, electrically dead vehicle. A hundred yards or less brought it to a standstill. Grabbing the children from the rear seat, Pauline hurried down the dark lane, not daring to look at her inquisitive, luminous 'companion'. The 'thing' had been with them now for some minutes. Arriving breathless at her house she burst through the front door, gasping half-completed sentences to her husband Billy about what had happened. He was disbelieving, but her eldest boy Clinton, aged sixteen, came with her to the front door and was just in time to see the thing fading away, travelling over the fields towards the sea.

Recovering her breath Pauline told Billy the car was 'buggered', and asked what she should do about getting to work the following day. She remembers, 'He hopped in the car, turned the key and the damn thing went first time', but the car was never right again after that day and was plagued with electrical trouble; so much so that they sold it within a few weeks.

Reviewing her reactions now, in the quiet security of her farmhouse and over a comforting cup of tea, had her behaviour seemed a bit panic-stricken? But as she said, 'We were scared stiff!'

It was a pity that the car was not still available for inspection, but apparently after that date, the direction indicators and the whole of the ignition system had been very temperamental. I recalled amongst other incidents the experience of Louise Bassett on 6 February and the trouble she had had with the radio interference; but she was nowhere near as close as Pauline Coombs to the supposed cause of it, the UFO.

Ripperston Farm is within half a mile of the Atlantic coast and is indeed the nearest property to the foreshore at this point, controlling some 400 acres of grazing. Billy Coombs is head herdsman, running the establishment virtually singlehanded. Clinton assists on the farm, while Pauline Coombs works in a local turkey factory. The nearest properties, half a mile distant, are Lower Broadmoor Farm, which is part of the same farming group, and Windmill Park; but the half-mile dirt road over which most of the frightening chase had occurred, serves only as access to the Coombs's farm and the neighbouring cottage occupied by Brian Class, who works away on another farm, and his wife Caroline, who is employed in an office in Haverfordwest. The location therefore was set in an unoverlooked and quite isolated spot in approximately one square mile of its own private land. There is no right of way through the farm and the only vehicles likely to use the track would be those directly servicing the dairy unit, namely the daily milk tanker which comes regularly every afternoon.

So cut off were the buildings that they had their own sewerage and water supply and were dependent on the outside world only for electricity. The farm was situated at 149 ft above sea level and commanded a very wide panoramic horizon in all directions. Pauline Coombs impressed us as a very sincere, unassuming woman, concerned mainly with the welfare of her husband and five children – three girls and two boys. I established that prior to her experiences she had had no interest in UFOs, science fiction or related matters and rather wished that the whole thing had not happened. She had not gone out of her way to seek the public eye, rather the reverse, but had been pestered by radio interviewers, journalists, and some Ufological fringe elements.

As we talked on, she relaxed further and began to relate the events that had happened after that first fateful 12 April. We now began to understand why she had been so hesitant in telling her story, for what had appeared in the popular press was only the tip of the iceberg. I knew that here lay a wealth of information, if only it could be uncovered, and that we were dealing not just with one isolated incident but were on the verge of something spectacular. We asked to return that evening after the children had gone to bed, and talking would be easier, without the 'helpful' interruptions from the younger members of the family.

We picked our way again out along the half-mile dirt road. Going back along the St Brides peninsula, towards Haverfordwest, the twelve miles of semi-deserted lanes took on a new significance. We found ourselves peering expectantly into the clear blue sky and viewing the innocent green countryside with a little more suspicion. We passed one shop and one petrol station, if you could call a single pump a petrol station.

'It's a bit out in the sticks, isn't it?' commented Jane.

2

The Giants Return

During the interview with Pauline Coombs she had suggested that we call on her nephew, Mark Marston, son of her brother Terry Marston, They live in St Margaret's Way, Herbrandston a few miles away, near to Milford Haven. Mark is a lively, somewhat boisterous twelve-year-old, intelligent and outwardgoing. Herbrandston is a small hamlet mostly of council-owned houses, neatly kept and set high on a hill overlooking the surrounding landscape. The family welcomed us warmly, and Terry, who has a very inquiring mind, quizzed me for information that might lead to some solution to his son's strange encounter.

The story was a fascinating one. On 15 April 1977, just three days after Pauline's first encounter with her 'flying football', Mark had been out looking for birds' eggs in the fields a few hundred yards from his home. It was evening and dusk had fallen, when Mark suddenly noticed, in the vicinity of a nearby silage container, a huge silver-suited figure. The 'man' was at least 6 ft tall and was completely enclosed in an aluminium-like suit, which seemed to be slightly inflated. He had boots, gloves, and a helmet which encased his head.

Mark remembers: 'It climbed easily over a big gate and when I started walking backwards it came towards me.' He ran, badly frightened, towards home, unnerved by the approaching giant.

Turning to glance over his shoulder at his pursuer, he remembers: 'It stopped underneath a street light and I could see that the head seemed to be square-shaped, with a black face. It had an aerial sticking up from one shoulder. It had flat black boots with no heels. I ran home as fast as I could. It looked to be well over 6 ft tall.'

Terry remembers well that his son had been very frightened, which is unusual, without there having been a very good cause.

A little later, Terry returned with his son to the scene of the encounter, armed with a torch, but could find no sign of the strange intruder. However, exactly where Mark had seen the figure jump off the gate, Terry found the clear outline of a huge footprint in the slurry. It showed a flat-soled boot, with no tread, about 12 in long; and there was a very strange characteristic, which is very revealing. The slurry of watery mud and cow dung would not normally bear the weight of a man's tread. Hence, in the normal way, if you or I had stepped on it, our feet would have sunk 4 or 5 inches into the mire and emerged leaving no clear imprint, just an unclear hole. But this footprint was no more than half an inch deep and clearly defined. As it seemed very unlikely that the man could have trailed his foot without placing his full weight on it – indeed it seemed to have been the foot upon which he had landed from the top of the three-foot-high gate – it indicated that by some strange method he had either been extremely light, or had not been affected by gravity to the same extent as one would expect.

So we had a strange set of conclusions to play with. Were we dealing with an individual who weighed no more than ten or twenty pounds, someone indeed so light that he was nearly on the point of floating; or possibly his suit had been filled with some very light gas which gave him an extra buoyancy. Alternatively, his suit incorporated some system which was giving him a high degree of upward lift. Mark had seen no apparatus, or 'jet pack', as used by American marines to hedge hop. Therefore we were left with something of a mystery as to how this effect had been achieved. According to Mark the figure had moved with agility and ease, despite his massive proportions, broad shoulders and generally stocky appearance. Exactly as to whether this was his true build or was due to the slightly puffy effect of his protective suit was not easy to determine. However, Mark claims to have seen a red glow in the field behind the figure and in the dusk the vague shape of an upside-down 'saucer'.

The red glow in the sky had also been noticed by Mark's mother Sandra and by a neighbour, Mrs Ivy John.

Terry revealed to me that his son had not been the only Herbrandston resident to have been visited by the 'other-worldly' figures. A good number of people in the village had been witness to some pretty scary incidents.

We crossed the road to a neat snowcemmed house and talked with Mr Swan. Apparently his daughter Debbie, aged thirteen, was one of five children who had seen a UFO not more than half a mile away from Mark's sighting, but two days later, on 17 April. As with Pauline Coombs, Debbie's UFO had been about the size of a football and had been hovering near a hedgerow. She remembers that it had been moving about in a very agitated fashion and the children had all run away from it. The football had been silver-coloured and had been observed in broad daylight. Other children in the village had also seen strange red glows in the vicinity.

When we returned to Terry's house he related another story from a local resident who was not prepared to discuss it, or would even admit that it had in fact taken place. The story is therefore to a degree hearsay, but knowing the circumstances, I personally believe it.

This young man had been returning home late one night from the local hostelry; therefore, in this one particular instance, cynics may well justifiably say that he may have had one too many. However, the story goes that, walking along a quiet and darkened country lane, he had come across a huge silver-suited figure. On this occasion the figure was not wearing a helmet and the witness was particularly struck by the large, slightly protruding eyes. Again, as in Mark's case, the figure had moved towards him and he was totally terrified – convinced that he had met the Devil himself. He ran headlong for home. His family remembers that he arrived in 'a terrible state', convinced that some retribution was about to be exacted from him for his sins.

This story was to be paralleled by a very similar description from a totally different witness (see chapter 6) in an entirely unconnected location, and therefore despite the circumstances I give the above some credence.

The village of Herbrandston is only four miles from the Coombs's farm at Ripperston, and the small hamlet virtually adjoins the extensive oil complex which spreads out in an ever growing area from Milford Haven. Also in the vicinity is the site for a new 'nutcracker' plant, an advanced process for utilizing highly volatile petro-chemical gases which would otherwise be lost and are at present burnt off. The new process involving these highly inflammable and explosive liquids will reduce the lost gases to a usable petrochemical product, and it is hoped that the plant will be operational by 1983. Whether the figure had any connection with this or the other related advanced technology in the area is open to speculation. However, the presence of the oil refineries nearby could be just a 'red herring'.

Everyday working-class people were not the only citizens to be observing UFOs in this early period. Just after Christmas 1976, Captain Timothy Sullivan, thirty-one-year-old son of Colonel and Mrs J. A. Sullivan, saw a strange low-flying object from the family home at Benton Castle. The family had kept the sighting quiet until late May and only revealed their experiences when other publicity showed that they were not the only people to observe this sort of thing. Captain Sullivan's mother, Mrs Elizabeth Sullivan, recalls that her son had just returned home from a dinner party when he observed the object flying low over the river Cleddau at about 1,000 miles per hour. It was a large circular shape, somewhat woolly in appearance and covered in lights. It gave the distinct impression that it was manned and Mrs Sullivan said that her son had not believed in UFOs before, but did so now. She commented, 'I'm longing to see one myself.'

Other sightings had occurred in the early spring, among them two in the month of May. Mr Dennis Thirkill of Pembroke saw a brilliant object one Thursday at four a.m.

He stated: 'At first I thought it was the morning star, then I realized that it couldn't be, northeast of me as it was. I went into the kitchen and looked at it through binoculars. Then I thought it could be an aircraft catching the sun, which was just beginning to come up. Then I saw aircraft and knew it couldn't be that.'

He called his wife and remembers, 'She wasn't too pleased at being woken but I wanted to make sure I wasn't seeing things; she saw it and then it suddenly disappeared. I was twenty-seven years in the services and I am something of a pragmatist,' he said.

The object appeared to have been pulsing at a distance of about three or four miles from him and he estimated that it must have been about fifty feet in width and travelling very slowly.

Another sighting, about the same period, was by a Milford Haven businessman from Thornton. This took the form of a silvery 'rugby ball' which was flying low over his home. It was observed for about four minutes as it travelled on a zigzag course in an easterly direction and appeared to have a dome on the top of the object, which he thought was about the size of an airliner. He studied it through binoculars, together with a neighbour, and was so amazed that he exclaimed, 'I have laughed about UFOs for ages, but this blasted object has changed my views completely. I'm not a nutcase, and I do believe my own eyesight. I've travelled the world quite a bit, and I've never seen anything like it before.'

There had been other fascinating information from the good people of Herbrandston, but I shall return to that later in another chapter specifically on electro-magnetic effects. Meanwhile, when we returned to Ripperston Farm that evening, the Coombs family related one of the most traumatic encounters of the whole period.

This was the first time we had met the other members of the Coombs family. Billy Coombs turned out to be a squat, jovial Welshman who took everything in his stride and hid a quiet serious mind behind a frontage of jokes and continuous leg pulling. His eldest son Clinton, aged sixteen, was a very quiet teenager. Kieron, only twelve years, was a typical, boisterous youngster full of his own ability and zealous youth. Both twins, Layanne and Joanne, were a little shy and took somewhat after their mother. All the family struck me as being intelligent and talented. Billy Coombs had been an accountant in the RAF many years previously and had also attended the University Veterinary College at Aberystwyth.

The dramatic incident, which had involved all the members of the family, had occurred shortly after midnight in the very early hours of Saturday, 24 April 1977. The children had gone to bed and Billy and Pauline were sitting up late watching the midnight film, a Western.

I should explain that the sitting-room of the Coombs's farmhouse has a single 3 ft-wide bay window in the centre of the front wall, and looking from inside, the television set is to the left of this bay in one corner of the room, a few feet along the wall in the middle of which is a large Welsh fireplace. Therefore, from outside the window, it is just possible to see the television, and the interior of the room. A large settee is placed directly opposite the fireplace, in view of the television, and to the left of this is an easy chair, which would be looking directly at the bay window. On this memorable evening Pauline had been sitting in the easy chair and Billy, as he was in the habit of doing, was laid out on the settee, resting his legs after the day's toil.

Late at night in the middle of the deserted countryside, outside the Coombs's farmhouse, it is as black as coal, with only the light from stars and the moon if the cloud cover allows. They have one exterior light which is not usually switched on unless they are working outside, and the lights of the farm complex are over 100 yards away.

Just before 1.00 a.m. Pauline noticed something silvery shimmering just outside the bay window in the front garden. It was moving about, but she was nervous to mention it to Billy on account of his sceptical attitude to her previous chase with the 'flying football'. The television started to act up, and the silvery shimmering outline was now closer to the window pane. Pauline was on the point of plucking up courage to mention it, when Billy, perhaps catching the movement out of the corner of his eye, glanced towards the window and leapt, startled, from his reclining position into a state of immediate alarm.

'Good God, what the hell is that?' yelled Billy.

Pauline recalled: 'We stood trembling, sweating and crying with fright.' For both of them were now staring through the window at a huge spacesuited individual standing but a few feet beyond in the darkness, caught dimly in the reflection of the interior lights of the room. There was nothing out there in the garden that could possibly give rise to an illusion, and as they watched, the figure shuffled closer towards them.

They backed away, Pauline clinging to Billy and nearly hysterical with fright. Billy recalls, 'It was definitely the shape of a man, but a terrible size, and so broad.' The television picture had now disintegrated into a chaotic zigzag of meaningless lines and overwhelming interference while the sash-window started to vibrate and rattle for no reason. The one single factor which alarmed them more than anything else was the superhuman size of their visitor. The bay window ended shortly before the ceiling, and the top of it must have been about 6 ft 6 in above the ground level of the footpath outside, but this figure towered above it, making him over 7 ft tall. He had exceptionally long arms, or so it seemed. He was clad completely in a one-piece silver aluminium-looking spacesuit, which extended into gloved hands of the same material and was capped by a square, solid-looking helmet that fitted right down to the shoulders. This was fronted by an opaque, black square visor, through which no facial features were discernible, and coming from the lower central point of the helmet was a thick, dark-coloured pipe which went back over his left shoulder.

From the visitor's position he could view the television and the terrified occupants of the room, and he remained motionless, observing the scene.

Blackie, the farmyard dog, usually a noisy and exuberant hound, circled his tail in one corner of the room, whimpering. Later he would not go out of the house.

The situation seemed to continue interminably, the figure standing quietly outside, almost motionless, and the couple inside too panic-stricken to think of any rational action. It

39

is very hard in these situations to estimate time but this continued for a good while. Pauline rushed upstairs and grabbed the children from their beds, fearing for their safety, and they remained huddled together on the opposite side of the room from the window, fearing to take their eyes off the individual lest he go round the house to another entrance; but he remained silent and inscrutable, just standing there seemingly fascinated by the black and white television receiver that was continuing to produce its zigzag of disjointed lines and 'white noise'. They noticed that the 'astronaut' was surrounded by a kind of luminous glow.

The figure moved back a little and, jolted into action by the slight breaking of the tension, Billy and Pauline rushed to the telephone in the rear kitchen and summoned police assistance. In disjointed sentences they tried to explain their 'other-worldly' situation. A confused and incredulous desk sergeant said that he would send a car to them, not knowing exactly what to expect.

Billy and Pauline also telephoned their boss Richard Hewison at the neighbouring farm, only half a mile to the northeast. He said he would come immediately, and some twenty minutes or so later, having hurriedly dressed, he was the first to arrive.

However, by this time, the figure had disappeared and the two confused police constables who arrived shortly afterwards could find no trace of the giant intruder. The television, the Western now ended, no longer registered interference, but it seemed to be faulty, and indeed it never worked properly again after that night. Only the following morning did they find any physical evidence of the previous night's incident. Outside the bay window at which the huge figure had stood, and only a few inches to one side of it, was a high rambling-rose bush, and on the side which was facing towards where the figure had been, all the leaves were mysteriously discoloured and burnt to a light brown crisp. The plant in later months did grow but the branches on that side never produced leaves or buds again.

The account of the reaction of the two police constables had also been interesting to me. Rather than being incredulous they had been the complete opposite, openly nervous and in fact politely declining to make a search of the farm, on the basis that they did not know what they were looking for. Apparently other officers from the same area had been involved in the occasional strange experience, and rather than writing the whole thing off, the police seemed definitely jumpy about investigating more than was absolutely necessary.

Collaboration came, however, from Josephine Hewison, who during the same night had noticed that her bedroom window was vibrating and rattling in the same inexplicable manner as the sash-windows over at the Coombs's farm. There was absolutely no wind and even when there was she had never noticed the window doing this before. Whatever apparatus or system the visitor had been using it certainly seemed to have been emitting a pretty strong electromagnetic and also sonic frequency to have caused these very physical effects. It was obvious that we were not dealing with any psychic spectre or mental hallucination, as I have never heard of a ghost blowing out a television set, even if the windows do rattle, in all the best Alfred Hitchcock movies.

In a subsequent interview with Mrs Hewison we learnt that she too had been 'close encountered', but a day or two after Pauline Coombs's first sighting on 12 April, and ten days previous to the window-rattling episode. She had sighted the 'thing' from the same bedroom window, when she was getting up one early morning, her husband Richard already being up and about the farm. Looking from the first-floor window she was amazed to see that beyond her extensive front garden, and just in front of the large greenhouse, there was resting on the grass a 50-ft-diameter 'flying saucer', that looked just like 'an upturned jellymould'.

She recalls: 'When I realized it wasn't from the farm, I thought it must be a UFO. I don't think it could have been

41

anything else. It was about ten to eight on a bright sunny morning. I went to the bedroom window and I saw this thing parked alongside the greenhouse. I wasn't in the least frightened. I just couldn't believe my eyes. I thought, what on earth is it doing by my greenhouse? It was silver colour, about 50 ft across the base and shaped like a jelly mould. It was as high as a double-decker bus. The greenhouse is 13 ft to the eaves but this towered above it. There was no movement; it had no visible windows or openings. I waited for something to emerge. It didn't. It went after ten minutes. It left no mark, not even a broken twig.'

The object she described was about 100 yards distant from her on the other side of a few low trees, and was identical to that observed by the Broad Haven schoolchildren earlier that year. One of her children thought that he had also seen something on a previous day but Mrs Hewison quietly commented, 'My first reaction to the children's story was that it was good for a laugh, but that's all. I didn't believe in flying saucers then, but I'm slightly less sceptical now.'

The following day we were to return again to Ripperston Farm, where Pauline had kindly agreed to show us where other encounters had taken place during the period since the appearance of her visitor at the window. It was heartening that she was now feeling at ease enough to open up about things that had never before been revealed beyond the confines of the family. So the morning found us again at the farm, walking down the track that leads from the dairy complex towards the sea over the large level fields.

She related that a few weeks later, in May 1977, she had sighted a landed UFO from her kitchen window on the seaward side which overlooks a large field of about 10 acres. The object was resting on the ground on a tripod undercarriage, about 400 or 500 yards distant from her, to the northeast. She thought it was roughly between about 14 ft to 20 ft in diameter and was approximately 3 ft off the ground. It was silvery coloured and had an antenna. Such was her familiarity with the farm tractors and equipment, there was no way she could have made a misidentification of one of these and anyway she would have known where the men had been working previously. The object had taken off and departed seawards.

When they inspected the field later they found a circular burn mark in the grass and a certain amount of soil displacement. I noticed that the ground was rather wet and Pauline's husband told me that the UFO site was exactly over a water-supply line, made of PVC and sunk about $2\frac{1}{2}$ ft underground, which runs across the field to supply cattle with drinking water. At this location was a right-angled junction with another branchline, and the ground was a little wet because the joint was leaking.

It was surely not coincidence that the UFO had chosen, of all the many acres, this exact point to come to rest. The waterlines which come down from the farm lead through this junction and out through water troughs in the fields used only by the cattle; hence the water supply from this point on would not be in domestic use. It was with some alarm to me personally, however, that he mentioned that a UFO investigator, with a geiger counter, had visited the site of the UFO landing and had found trace radiation indications from the burned circle. It was likely that the radiation noted had not been from a dust but had originated from the ground, having been irradiated by a radioactive source. A later test showed that the radiation had faded, being no more than the normal 'background count'.

We walked on over the fields, the bright blue waters of the Atlantic stretched out before us now from our high elevation on the cliffs more than 123 ft above the foreshore just 300 yards farther on to the northeast. We stopped at the entrance to the field that adjoins the coastline and here, with the valuable aid of the twins, Pauline and her children described another incident.

Joanne and Layanne had been out together playing in this field which had been put to hay, with thickly sown grass,

43

when up from the nearby rocky beach had walked in broad daylight another of the giant spacesuited figures. He had approached the twins, slightly on a line to one side of them, at a steady but slightly stiff gait, and had passed within about 12 ft of them as they crouched too frightened to run away. The description of him was identical to that of the figure who had waited that dark night at Pauline's sitting-room window, and he had also had the breathing-tube coming from the front of the black square visor. He left clear indentations in the grass but, strangely, rather than going through the open gateway near to the children and at the top of the field he jumped over the barbed wire fence and hedgerow only 15 ft or 20 ft to the left of the entrance. He had done this with such incredible athletic ease that there is no way in which it could have been achieved without some mechanical aid. Upon reaching the other side and the field in which the UFO had landed over the waterline previously, he walked up the field towards that spot and then turned northeastwards and in a curving line walked down again to the coastal path leading to Mill Haven, where he disappeared down into the cove and was not seen again. The twins suffered no ill effects from the encounter, neither did it seem that the figure had taken any notice of them, despite passing within only 4 yards of them and surely having seen them.

It seemed to be a general reaction with these figures that contrary to the norm of avoiding adults, they took no notice of children, probably regarding them as no threat to their presence.

We returned slowly to the house, discussing all the various implications of the intense interest aroused by the figures in this very small area of Welsh countryside. Again we settled over a cup of tea and this time with the aid of sturdy little Kieron, he and Layanne excitedly, and with some interruption from each other, described what to me was so far the most revealing of all the incidents.

The two children had again been down near the cliffs and

the same field where the silver figure had walked, when they had seen three UFOs in the sky. They were again dome-shaped and circular; and the possibility of their having had some kind of porthole or markings on them was debated between the children. One of the UFOs was extremely low, probably at a height of less than 50 ft, while the second remained stationed a few hundred yards higher to one side and the third was just a bright speck in the sky high overhead. The lowest of the craft had dropped what to all appearances was a metal ladder of some description and one of the silver-suited figures descended this to the field. This time the sighting seemed to have occurred a little more to the west, nearer the hedgerow which divides this from the next field along the coast.

The lowest UFO had now dropped a bright red fluorescent 'box,' which apparently fell in the long grass, although they were not sure exactly where. When the figure had returned to his vehicle, and all the craft had flown off seawards, the two children had run excitedly into the field to try and find 'the red box'. But despite an hour's diligent searching in the long grass they could find no trace of it.

Kieron had been searching about with his hands and Layanne had been kicking about with her feet. Next day Pauline was very alarmed to find that Kieron's arms and hands and Layanne's knees, shins and feet had become swollen, with blotchy red patches, and despite a visit to the doctor, no logical cause could be found other than the possibility of some unknown allergy. The patches disappeared after three or four days and have never recurred.

Whether they were in fact a simple reaction to the hay, which seems highly unlikely as the children are often in the fields and play about the farm continuously without any similar reaction, or whether the children had been affected by some unidentified radiation or even virus or bacteria was never determined. They showed no sign of the patches now. There was also the suggestion that the children might have had a tummy upset; whether this was due to their contact or just eating too much dinner could not be determined either at this late date.

So, to assemble what we had so far, the UFOs and their occupants were taking an unnatural interest in Ripperston Farm and in the fields on the coastal side of it. Either because they could not breathe the atmosphere, or to protect them from something as yet unknown, they were wearing totally protective suits, even to the extent of heavily tinted visors, which might suggest that their eyes were not capable of standing normal sunlight. Their interest in the innocuous PVC waterlines was at this stage a complete mystery but it did seem likely that within a few hundred yards of the Coombs's home they had planted some sophisticated automatic device, 'the red box', that the children had failed to find but had come so close to. There was the possibility of trying to locate it with sophisticated apparatus, but it felt rather like searching for a black cat in a dark hole. Perhaps subconsciously I didn't want to find it. We were dealing with an unknown quantity, and some physical danger might ensue to anybody digging it up.

There were other patterns about which one had mixed feelings. The Broad Haven children and villagers had seen their UFO on two occasions near the school, but it had also been near the sewage-processing works, which I learnt later recycles effluent water into drinking water, so one wondered in which particular facility the UFO's crew were interested. Was it the school, the schoolchildren, the sewerage or the drinking water? It could have been all or either or none of these. To state that Mark Marston had seen his giant figure near a farm silage silo seemed to be grabbing at straws and I felt that beyond all of these facts lay something else we had not as yet discovered which would in some way tie all the little pieces together into a coherent picture. That picture was slowly emerging but it would not come out of a quick weekend trip to Wales. It was to take months and months of digging and painstaking collection of seemingly irrelevant facts until the final startling truth was revealed.

46

We determined that other than in the next few days we would have to return for a detailed survey later in the autumn and try to discover the truth. Meanwhile we were to learn by our other interviews on this trip that there were forces at work whose objective was the very reverse of this and that whatever it was we were trying to discover was so 'hot', so secret, and such a powder-keg, that considerable effort would be made to withhold the facts from the general public and the local residents. What had started as a relatively innocent investigation into the UFOs was to take on a more sinister and much more significant meaning.

It is said in the Bible that 'in those days there were giants in the Earth'. Now the giants had returned, and it would seem that they had done so with some intentness and alarm. What could possibly be happening in this remote and isolated corner of West Wales that should attract so much unprecedented attention? The oil refineries in nearby Milford Haven had been there for many years, and despite the planned expansion there seemed no reason for a sudden influx of special interest.

The area was directly underneath the principal airlanes for jet traffic between Europe and the eastern States of the United States and New York, but there seemed no special significance in this fact either, and anyway the Jumbos at this particular point on the route would be flying many miles high, visible only as distant contrails in the clear blue.

We were dealing with a very insular community, one reluctant to talk, in which facts were circulated only inside family and community limits. Fortunately we had been accepted into this family and the unrelated pieces of fascinating information that its individual members held were building together into a picture which extended far beyond this small Welsh community, both outwards and, it seemed, upwards.

3

The Great UFO Cover-up

The appearance of the silversuited giants was not restricted to the back yard of Ripperston Farm or indeed to this one small corner of Wales. In February 1977, Vera Partington, of Harrow, Middlesex had reported to me an encounter with a very similar figure on the road between Wealdstone and Harrow Weald, one winter's evening at 10.30. She was driving from Harrow Weald to her home at Harrow-on-the-Hill, along the darkened road, when her car's headlights picked out a huge silversuited man.

She vividly remembers: 'He was walking down the centre of the footpath, going in our direction, wearing what looked like a silver, all-in-one wet suit or diver's suit. He was about 6 ft tall and on the top of his helmet was what appeared to be an aerial about 8 in high. His walk seemed to be a sort of dogged plodding, with his arms swinging about a foot away from his body. I turned round quickly to catch a glimpse of his front, but too late, we were round the bend of the road and out of sight.'

The drawing that she supplied of her 'spaceman' showed that he had a helmet coming down to his shoulders, encasing his head, in exactly the same manner as the figures in Wales. What he could have been doing or where he was going, just on the edge of Greater London, remains a mystery, but at the same time reports of UFOs, carrying multi-coloured lights, came in from all over the Watford and St Albans area. One might comment that Miss Partington was witness to something of a harrowing experience.

Also during February 1977 more reports came in from the London area. Mr Fletcher of Belvedere wrote to me: 'I have had two experiences of UFOs. The first was in October 1976. I was driving home late one night after dropping my girlfriend off and had travelled about 100 yards up the road when I noticed this star coming towards me, but as it got closer I noticed it was not one star but two, slightly apart and emitting a brilliant blue and white light.

'I thought to myself, Oh! it's one of those UFO things, and flashed my headlights on and off at it. I regret doing that to this day. After that it veered off at incredible speed away from me, in the direction I was going. By the time I had got to the roundabout it was hovering about 40 ft above the ground – as I got halfway round, the engine just died on me – I turned the ignition but there was nothing, not even a slight turn from the starter motor.

'It seemed to be playing a cat and mouse game with me, and I was the mouse. After what seemed ages it moved away slowly this time, but there was no noise from it at all. I turned the ignition and the car started first time and I completed the roundabout and put my foot down on the dual carriageway. I thought I had lost it but it came over the top of the highest Thamesmead flats and began to run parallel to my car, but I had the advantage this time because it had to dodge several electric pylons and change course.

'I looked out of the window and saw it had stopped and seemed to be hovering again, but I did not worry about that, I drove to the nearest police station and reported it. I thought they would laugh and say I was a crank, but the officer on duty said two of his men had reported seeing strange lights shooting across the sky that night.

'The second experience was about three weeks ago. It was getting dark and I was just finishing working on my car, when a car pulled up at the top of the road. The occupants, an elderly couple, were pointing in the direction of the park. There was this object that had chased me previously, flashing and lighting up an area of the park. I watched it for some time but as I turned to go back indoors, to my astonishment there was a formation of six travelling north.

'I drove around to my friend's and we rushed out into the

back garden armed with a powerful pair of night-lensed binoculars and a camera with only two shots left on the film. They stayed in formation for about another five minutes, then broke off in different directions, only to be joined by another which was different from the others, being much larger. I would have estimated it in the region of 100 ft long, and it had what seemed to be red and green flashing lights.

'The "mother ship", if we call it that, stayed on a south course while the other six seemed to stop at different points of interest and then move on. At one time one of the craft passed over the houses at a height of approximately 150 ft. I viewed it through the binoculars and saw that between the two lights it was cigar-shaped and had something on top of it.

'They stayed for about another half an hour surveying points of interest before vanishing out of sight. We took photographs of the larger object, but have not had them developed yet. I have never told anyone of these experiences, probably because they would never believe me, but I am quite sane, I assure you.'

Unfortunately, lighting conditions were too dark for Mr Fletcher's film to record the UFOs and the film came out blank, but the theme of surveying specialist installations continued with a rash of over fifty sightings at Telford, Shropshire. Twenty of these had been made by council workers constructing a new sewerage works there.

Terry Billington, a member of the Telford Council Engineering Department, remembers: 'I saw a metallic saucer-shaped disc hovering over farmland. The only thing that was in view apart from green fields was the sewerage works. The disc finally flew off much faster than any aeroplane. I'm not a UFO addict, and wasn't interested in them until this happened. In fact I describe myself as "very down to earth".'

The UFO interest in our pollution problems seemed quite intense; and Mr Billington was not the only highly qualified person to be reporting UFOs around the world. In a remarkably frank and openminded report, the Spanish Air Ministry in Madrid released the following information on 11 July 1976, describing apparently only one of many similar incidents recorded in their files. This event had been witnessed by none other than General Carlos Cavero, the Commanding Officer of the Spanish Air Force in the Canary Islands. He was on the Spanish mainland, driving near the village of Sabada in a remote region of eastern Spain, when his amazing sighting occurred.

He describes: 'It was giving off a brilliant light, and it travelled at an extraordinary speed. As an Air Force officer I hold, officially, the same opinions as the Air Ministry. But personally, I think these unidentified flying objects come from other planets.'

General Cavero estimated that the object he had observed took only two seconds to traverse the distance between two villages which he knew to be twelve miles apart. There seems to be some doubt that this timing is strictly accurate; for if it had taken only two seconds its speed would have been 23,760 miles per hour, which is faster than the velocity of most satellites.

His report, however, had been followed the next day by an amazing observation by a well-respected doctor, Francisco Padron, who had seen an object while he was motoring towards Tenerife, in the Canary Islands.

He recounted: 'It was nearly dark, and I was driving along a lonely road. Then I saw a round sphere, about 40 ft in diameter, hovering above the road ahead of me. It was emitting a bluish light and was about 20 ft above the ground. As I approached, my radio cut out, but my headlights kept working. I passed right underneath and saw, silhouetted inside, through a type of porthole, two very tall figures dressed in bright red. Then it took off and vanished.'

The same openminded official attitude did not seem to be shared by the Ministry of Defence in London. Referring to a sighting made over Leigh in Essex a spokesman for the Ministry had stated that they had investigated the observation by three Essex police officers, but refused to comment on their findings.

PC Richard Rowley described the object as 'cigar-shaped, very bright with an orange tint'.

Mr Shaw, a former RAF storeman, first glimpsed the object dropping through clouds. Then PC Malcolm Young of Leigh police and his colleague Richard Rowley had observed the object for about five minutes and again fifteen minutes later. Twenty-four-year-old PC Rowley stated: 'Malcolm first pointed it out and we stopped the car to look at it. We watched it for about five minutes and then drove back towards the station. When we got back to the station, Malcolm's wife said she had seen it too.'

Why the Ministry refused to comment is conjecture or perhaps they were just snowed under with reports which they could not explain. These had included a strange ring of flashing lights which buzzed aircraft over Heathrow airport and a flashing red light observed by two pilots which overtook them as they neared Southend.

Generally speaking, I find that the British police force is very openminded about the subject of UFOs, and to further my investigation in western Wales I took myself along to Haverfordwest police station, where I quizzed the local force for their reaction. The visit was surprisingly successful. Of the few men gathered in the office, three had actually seen UFOs themselves. Everybody accepted the reality of the phenomenon; indeed the question of its unreality seemed laughable. They had received many reports from the general public of objects in the area, building to an ever increasing climax through 1977.

One such report had come from twelve-year-old Mark Jones and his friend Glen Evans, who were walking to their Youth Club on 19 December 1976, when they saw an object hovering over the Welsh National Water Development Authority Offices at Haverfordwest.

Mark saw a woman passer-by looking up, and he reported: 'I looked as well and saw an object like two saucers together, divided by a yellow and green line. At first Glen could not see it. Then when he did we both ran over to tell his father. I saw it again, but the next time we looked round it had disappeared. But it was definitely there. I must have seen it for at least a minute.' They both ran and immediately reported their sighting to the local police.

Another report to the police had come from children and teenagers who had seen a UFO, emitting flames, landing on a nearby beach late one evening in 1976.

When questioned as to the procedure for dealing with these matters, the desk sergeant, with an expression I find difficult to describe, looked at me and said simply: 'There *is* no procedure, sir.'

Nothing further needed to be said. The authorities seemed faced with a situation for which no provision had ever been made, and because no provision had ever been made, no provision could be made. It seemed, officially, it did not exist. The parting comment was made by Detective Inspector Charlton, who said quietly: 'After what I've seen round here, nothing would surprise me.'

The position of the British police seemed similar to that of their colleagues in the United States. Neither police force had been given any instructions as to how to deal with UFO reports, and indeed the respective Ministries of Defence, or their agents, seemed indirectly to discourage the involvement of the civilian police, apparently considering the matter as remaining strictly within the domain of 'national security'. This had been highlighted by new information released under the Freedom of Information Act in the United States. This early, but significant, information highlighted the disorganization, and the restricting specialist roles that each individual agency had adopted from the beginning of the flying saucer reports. It also serves as a complete denial to those who maintain that the UFOs are some American or even Russian secret weapon which was invented shortly after the end of the Second World War, for the documents clearly show that the American administration was in complete confusion over the issue.

On 7 October 1947 the FBI filed the following memorandum on the subject of 'Flying Discs'.

At request of Brigadier General George F. Schulgen, Chief of the Requirements Intelligence Branch of Army Air Corps Intelligence, Special Agent . . . [name crossed off: call him 'SA'] discussed the above captioned matter [i.e. flying discs] with him on 9 July 1947. General Schulgen indicated to 'SA' that the air corps has taken the attitude that every effort must be undertaken in order to run down and ascertain whether or not the flying discs are a fact and, if so, to learn all about them. According to General Schulgen, the Air Corps Intelligence are utilizing all of their scientists in order to ascertain whether or not such a phenomenon could in fact occur. He stated that this research is being conducted with the thought that the flying objects might be a celestial phenomenon with the view that they might be a foreign body mechanically devised and controlled.

General Schulgen also indicated to 'SA' that all Air Corps installations had been alerted to run out each reported sighting to obtain all possible data to assist in this research project. In passing, General Schulgen stated that an Air Corps pilot who believed that he saw one of these objects was thoroughly interrogated by General Schulgen and scientists, as well as a psychologist, and the pilot was adamant in his claim that he saw a flying disc.

General Schulgen advised 'SA' that the possibility exists that the first reported sightings of a so-called flying disc were fallacious and prompted by individuals seeking personal publicity, or were reported for political reasons. He stated that if this was so, that subsequent sightings might be the result of mass hysteria. He pointed out that the thought exists that the first reported sighting might have been by individuals of communist sympathies with the view to causing hysteria and fear of a secret Russian weapon.

General Schulgen indicated to 'SA' that he is desirous of having all the angles covered in this matter. He stated that reports of his scientists and findings of various Air Corps installations would be available in his office. He advised that to complete the picture he desired the assistance of the Federal Bureau of Investigation in locating and questioning the individuals who first sighted the so-called flying disc in order to ascertain whether or not they are sincere in their statements that they saw these discs, or whether their statements were prompted by personal desire for publicity or political reasons. General Schulgen assured 'SA' that there were no War Department or Navy Department research projects presently being conducted which could in any way be tied up with the 'flying discs'. General Schulgen indicated to 'SA' that if the Bureau would co-operate with him in this matter, he would offer all the facilities of his office as to results obtained in the effort to identify and run down this matter.

'SA' advised General Schulgen that his request would be made known to the Bureau and an answer be made available to him as soon as possible.

'SA' also discussed this matter with Colonel L. R. Forney of MID. Colonel Forney indicated that it was his attitude that in as much as it had been established that the 'flying discs' are not a result of any Army or Navy experiment, the matter is of interest to the FBI. He stated that he was of the opinion that the Bureau, if at all possible, should accede to General Schulgen's request.

J. E. Hoover, director of the FBI at the time, was in full knowledge of this request and subscribed to the memorandum this note:

'I would do it but before agreeing to it we must insist upon full access to discs recovered. For instance, in the LA case, the Army grabbed it and would not let us have it for cursory examination.'

A week later another memorandum was filed which indicated that Hoover's decision had been advised to the Air Force:

This is to advise that 'SA' has recontacted General Schulgen and advised him in connection with the Director's notation. General Schulgen indicated to 'SA' that he desired to assure Mr Hoover of complete cooperation in this matter and stated that he would issue instructions to the Field directing that all co-operation be furnished to the FBI and that all discs recovered be made available for examination by the FBI agents. General Schulgen pointed out to 'SA' that he will from time to time make the results of the studies of his scientists available to the Bureau for the assistance of the FBI field offices. General Schulgen indicated to 'SA' that there had been a decrease in the reported sightings of discs which might be because of the fact that it has lost much of its publicity value. He indicated, however, that he believed it necessary to follow this matter through to determine as near as possible if discs were in fact seen and to determine their origin.

Co-operation between the two agencies continued for a month or two but by the autumn of 1947 relations were wearing thin and were typified by the following communications:

I am transmitting herewith copies of a 'restricted' letter dated 3 September 1947, which was furnished to me by ... [name not given] which letter is designated to certain Commanding Generals on the Army Air Forces from Colonel R. H. Smith, Assistant Chief of Staff – Intelligence, Headquarters Air Defence Command, Mitchelfield, New York, concerning 'co-operation of FBI and AAF on investigations of "flying disc" incidents'.

It is my understanding from recent Bureau instructions that we are to assist the Air Force intelligence personnel in the investigation of flying disc incidents. However, it will be noted from the attached letter that it is Army interpretation that it was their intent that the Bureau would investigate those incidents of the so-called 'discs' being found on the ground and apparently not those which are observed only in flight. Further, the attention of the Bureau is respectfully called to paragraph two of this letter and to the last sentence therein which states, 'the services of the FBI were enlisted in order to relieve the numbered Air Forces of the task of tracking down all the many incidences which turned out to be ash-can covers, toilet seats and whatnot'.

In the first place, the instructions issued by the Army Air forces in this letter appear to limit the type of investigations which the Bureau will be asked to handle and secondly it appears to me the wording of the last sentence of the second paragraph mentioned above is cloaked in entirely uncalled-for language tending to indicate the Bureau will be asked to conduct investigations only in those cases which are not important and which are almost, in fact, ridiculous.

The thought has occurred to me the Bureau might desire to discuss this matter further with the Army Air Forces both as to the types of investigations which we will conduct and also object to the scurrilous wordage which, to say the least, is insulting to the Bureau in the last sentence of paragraph two.

The above letter was sent to assistant director D. M. Ladd of the FBI and constituted a summary of the situation to Hoover.

The Ladd memorandum to Hoover was as follows:

The Bureau was requested by the Air Forces Intelligence to assist in attempting to arrive at an explanation of the 'Flying Disc'. The Air Forces indicated that the alleged sightings of flying discs might have been made by individuals of communist sympathies for the purpose of causing mass hysteria in the United States over a fear of the Secret Russian Weapon. The Bureau agreed to assist in the investigation of the reported sightings, and the Field was advised in Bureau bulletin 42, Series 1947 dated 30 July 1947, that they should investigate each instance which was brought to their attention of the sighting of a flying disc in order to ascertain whether or not it was a bona-fide sighting, an imaginary one, or a prank. The results of the investigation by the Bureau Field officer in this matter have failed to reveal any indications of subversive individuals being involved in any of the reported sightings.

Ladd's memorandum to the Director continued in conclusion:

'It is recommended that the Bureau protest vigorously to the Assistant Chief of Air Staff – 2. It is also recommended that the Bureau discontinue all activity in this field and that the Bureau Field Offices be advised to discontinue all investigations and to refer all complaints received to the Air Forces.

Two days later Hoover wrote to Major General George C. McDonald, Assistant Chief of Air Staff–2 at the Pentagon:

The Federal Bureau of Investigation has been requested by your office to assist in the investigation of the reported sightings of flying discs.

My attention has been called to instructions disseminated by the Air Forces relative to this matter. I have been advised that these instructions indicate that the Air Forces would interview responsible observers while the FBI would investigate incidents of discs found on the ground, thereby relieving the Air Forces of running down incidents which in many cases turned out to be 'ash-can covers, toilet seats and whatnot'.

In view of the apparent understanding by the Air Forces of the position of the Federal Bureau of Investigation in this matter, I cannot permit the personnel and time of this organization to be dissipated in this manner.

I am advising the Field Division of the Federal Bureau of Investigation to discontinue all investigative activity regarding the reportive sightings of flying discs, and am instructing them to refer all complaints received to the appropriate Air Force representative in their area.

[Signed] John Edgar Hoover, Director

Hence in America by the early days of autumn 1947 the FBI, due to tricky relations with the Army Air Force Intelligence at the Pentagon had effectively completely removed themselves from UFO investigation, and the matter falling within military circles had automatically become classified.

In Britain the state of the game seemed somewhat similar. If liaison did occur between the military and the police it was certainly not by previous procedure and only by off-chance communication. The continuing situation therefore exists that vast amounts of information, and the knowledge of a possible threat to the security of both countries – the United States and the United Kingdom – goes completely unregistered and officially ignored by the very members of society that are likely to be in touch with the grass roots.

It is highly significant that in the communications mentioned it seems accepted by the Army Air Intelligence Corps that the celestial discs are mechanically controlled vehicles from outer space, and it is also clearly stated that neither are they originating from any United States research programme nor are they a politically contrived hoax by communist agents. Assuming that the FBI are very thorough, as they usually are in their investigations, one must therefore assume, and indeed it was clearly stated at the time, that all of the UFO witnesses interviewed during their investigations turned out to be completely genuine. This has always been the pattern. Other than the odd hoax and occasional nutcase, it continues in this pattern to this day, as shown in the contents of the previous two chapters. But, returning to our local situation in West Wales, the scenario repeated itself: this time and some thirty years further on, with slightly more sinister overtones.

Our investigations took us on to another major witness, and indeed a whole new turn of events in the story.

Just outside the picturesque coastal village of Little Haven, the Haven Fort Hotel sits high on the cliffs, commanding a stupendous view over the waters of St Brides Bay. Aptly named, the hotel is a former castle or fort dating back many hundreds of years and still retaining its high battlements, arched Gothic windows, and arrow slits. No finer setting for a weird story could have been imagined.

The hotel is owned and run by Rose Granville and her family, husband Hayden and daughter Francine. Rose is of Spanish origin and with her English husband she moved to the hotel some years ago from Cardiff, where she had run a chain of boutiques. The building was converted into a two-star luxury hotel and now offers first-class accommodation to those visiting this unique old-world fishing village.

Rose has carefully retained and augmented the fantastic atmosphere of the building, and the place bristles with suits of armour and ancient weaponry. The rooms are set out in their original medieval style. When purchasing the hotel, Rose automatically found herself landlord of an estate which included the cliffs and beach in front of the hotel, much of the land around it and some offshore islands.

We found Rose to be a voluble, bustling lady in her forties, confident and experienced in the ways of the world. She had been in business all her life and had intended to make this her final home, but due to the events that had transpired she was now having some slight misgivings.

It had all started in April 1977. Hayden Granville was outside the hotel in the car park with some guests, when all of them observed a strange procession of lights across the sky. It was a clear evening, with the first stars visible. The lights were clearly separated and exactly following each other's tracks. There was absolutely no noise, neither were there any contrails and anyway the lights were too bright to be ordinary aircraft navigation lights. They were steady yellow and not flashing. All of the observers watched as the lights processed across the sky and disappeared to the northeast.

'It was just like watching a train in the sky, but only the windows, not the carriages,' said Hayden.

No explanation could be found for the phenomenon and other than its being thought unusual, the event passed without much comment.

A few nights later, towards the end of the month, the Granville family were to take the subject of UFOs far more seriously.

It was 2.30 a.m. and Rose Granville was about to retire to bed, being the last member of the family to do so, after having completed a hard day's work in the hotel. The early morning was pitch black, but the weather was fine. As she walked to her bedroom at the rear of the hotel down the long corridor, she was suddenly amazed to find that outside it was light as day. The car park is at the front of the building and there are only a few low-powered exterior lights at the rear so there was no explanation for this sudden brilliance.

She rushed to the window, curious and slightly alarmed. To her amazement she could see at about 200 yards to the east, near the perimeter of her 3-acre field, a strange craft hovering and illuminating the area underneath it with a cone-shaped light, the colour of an oxyacetylene welding-torch flame, a brilliant blue-white. The whole area for hundreds of yards around was clearly visible, but despite the obvious power of the device there was absolutely no sound, in fact an uncanny silence prevailed over the area. She could see clearly that the large machine was dome-shaped, faintly illuminated against the back reflection, and about 20 yards

61

from her far hedge. It was hovering over an area of grass which is completely unobstructed and has clear visibility on all sides. Just to the northeast of the craft's position, but 30 yards away, over the other side of her perimeter hedge, is a Royal Observer Corps nuclear fall-out shelter, to be used in the event of an atomic war for monitoring the levels of radiation present in the atmosphere. This was separated from the UFO's position only by a low 6 ft-high hedge and a row of 450-volt power cables which run along the line of the hedge.

However, none of these facts seemed relevant to Rose as she stood petrified, observing this other-worldly craft hovering over her backyard. Only later did the proximity of the government-owned installation appear significant; but now at this moment her only feelings were of fear and panic.

The situation became worse, for suddenly emerging from out of the underside of the craft came two fully spacesuited individuals who, to her amazement, walked through the brilliant blue-white flames. They were huge in proportion and were entirely encased in silver-like garments with a square dark-tinted visor entirely covering the face. They looked human, but of giant proportions, and they moved easily over the thick turf. Walking away from the craft in separate directions for a few yards they then bent down.

She remembers: 'They looked like human beings, and yet they didn't. They seemed to be trying to measure something.'

Throughout the episode the craft remained stationary, the light from the object pulsating gently in a rhythmical fashion. One of the figures stood up and looked in her direction, and with fear grabbing at her mind Rose suddenly realized that she was silhouetted in the large glass window which was clearly visible and outlined by the light from the craft. She ran, not knowing what to do, towards her bedroom to wake her husband and summon assistance, and half asleep and not fully appreciating the situation Hayden arrived at the window some few minutes later – only to find the craft had gone.

Rose breathed a deep sigh – it wasn't there any more.

The Granvilles were relieved for they did not want any more tales of ghosts and folklore being spread about the hotel. They had found in the six years that they had been there that old legends of its being haunted had affected trade and although throughout all of their occupation they had not seen a single spectre or any indication of the legends being true, the presence of the UFO was not welcomed. In the grounds of the hotel lay a prehistoric monolith in the form of a huge stone slab, face down and partly buried in the turf on the seaward side of the fort, which did not help matters in a community riddled with rumour and superstition; and it was said that the castle was walked by a 'white lady'. It was therefore their decision to say nothing about their strange encounter, indeed to keep it strictly to themselves lest it affect their hotel trade.

However, if Rose and Hayden were prepared to forget the UFOs, the UFOs were certainly not prepared to forget them or their property, and only a few nights after, when Rose was again late at night locking up the hotel and walking across the car park on the seaward side, she found herself suddenly confronted with a brilliant light in the sky. This time it was not as close as before, although its appearance was similar; but the light was more yellowish. It was moving over the hotel and then away over the nearby village of Little Haven along the coast towards the west. Rose Granville was filled with a mixture of emotions, something of curiosity, fear, expectation and bewilderment all rolled into one. She stood watching the light as it reached a point along the coast over some islands that she owned, and then, having paused for a moment, returned towards Little Haven and her position.

The hour was late, and the local conservative church-fearing community were all in bed. No one else was about. Rose recalls worrying that hotel residents might see the light, or even her standing there in the car park and think her behaviour very strange. The light did not seem to threaten her, but why wouldn't it go away?

If only it would go away!

But it did not go away and she watched it for forty-five minutes as it moved slowly and methodically up and down the coast, returning to the islands, then again back to the village, again to the islands. Back to the village, its path seemed monotonous and rigorously straight, its presence a mystery, its passage unnoticed by the sleeping community. This time Rose did not call her husband and she hardly mentioned the incident, but it was affecting her health. She could not sleep at nights; she kept worrying about it.

She could not even quietly resign herself that she might be seeing things, for on the day following the 'visit' in her rear field both she and her husband had examined the ground over which the craft had hovered. Clearly defined in the green turf had been a crescent-shaped, sharp depression, with some of the grass burnt black. No cars had been in the field, no bonfires had been lit, there was no explanation other than that the craft must have landed or at least caused the strange mark by its presence.

Since that fearful night other strange things had plagued her mind. The northern wing of the hotel is an old cottage, surmounted by ramparts, fallen into some disrepair and used only as a storeroom. During a recent rainfall it had suddenly started leaking, and concerned for the structure she had called upon the services of a local builder to inspect the roof. He had reported to her a perplexing discovery: on the far uppermost corner of the roof an area of about 3 ft in diameter had been affected by intense heat, and he asked her if there had been a fire in the building.

There was no evidence of there having been a fire, and none of the interior of the cottage had been damaged in any way, but this strange 3-ft circle of blue Welsh slates overlaid with bitumen had been so badly affected that the bitumen had burnt and run and the slates had cracked in the intensity of the temperature to which they must have been exposed. Neither had there been a storm or lightning strike.

Rose accordingly had the roof repaired, this time with cement, not the inflammable bitumen. The building and fire-alarm systems were inspected also for any possible fault or defect.

She regrets that a few days later, when she was confiding her experiences to one of the local visiting fire officers, the story leaked out and suddenly she was visited by UFO investigators and her name and story were in the local press. Fortunately it seems that the news headlines have not affected her business despite her fears, but this was not the end of her experiences, only the beginning, and her anxieties grew.

She recalls, 'I don't know what it is but I was petrified. If I see it again I am definitely moving from here.'

The proximity of the Royal Observer Corps nuclear fall-out shelter pressed upon her mind and she decided to write to her Member of Parliament complaining about her harassment by the strange and inexplicable events, even half suspecting that the Royal Observer Corps or some military or government agency was responsible for having caused them. Accordingly she dispatched a letter in early May 1977 and determined not to find herself again outside the security of her fortress late at night, fearing a further encounter with the strange pulsating lights.

One night, a short time after, she found herself again uncannily drawn to the window of the hotel at the end of a corridor overlooking St Brides Bay. She emphasized to me that she is far too busy a woman to waste time staring out of hotel windows, and she usually walked at night directly from her work to her bedroom to retire. In fact, as she said to me, 'I have grown so used to the view that I do not really look at it as much as the visitors do, I'm not all that keen on the sea anyway.'

But this night she again found herself staring through the darkness and there beyond, by the far cliffs, was this strange red disc glowing and undulating with a gentle pendulum-like movement. It must have been no higher than 100 ft above the water and again was only a short distance from her island; also in that direction was Ripperston Farm, home of the Coombs family and scene of their own strange encounters.

So used had she become now to the occurrences that although she remained afraid, they did not alarm her in the same way as at first.

Days went by and the Granvilles waited for their Member of Parliament, Nicholas Edwards, to do something, anything about it. Then things started to happen. The Ministry of Defence telephoned a couple of times, then the RAF, to make appointments. At last the mystery might be resolved.

The day came as arranged and outside on the gravel of the hotel car park a neatly painted RAF Land Rover crunched gently to a stop. The RAF driver waited, while a smartly dressed uniformed officer dismounted complete with black briefcase. He came alone, without assistants or entourage, and Mrs Granville was delighted to find that he was a Squadron Leader from the local RAF Brawdy.

Rather than dismissing her account as a hallucination he sat in her lounge for several hours meticulously filling up forms by hand and taking down every detail of her encounter. He seemed fascinated and intrigued, but not forthcoming. At the end of it all Mrs Granville felt that nothing really had been achieved and she asked him point blank for his own opinion.

He declared that he was openminded on the subject but in confidence he stated one thing categorically to her, and this she recalls clearly. 'He said there was absolutely nothing at RAF Brawdy that could possibly account for my sighting of the UFO, nothing they had there looked like this or could produce such a report. He asked me not to say anything about the incident to anyone, as he thought it was best not to alarm the general public.'

The Granvilles were not looking for publicity anyway, but they did not feel fully satisfied. The RAF could offer no explanation, and Rose's property had been damaged unaccountably. And now they were asking her to keep the whole thing secret and not tell anyone about it. She felt they knew more than they were telling and she pressured more. The end result was two letters, one from Nicholas Edwards MP and one from the Ministry of Defence. They read as follows:

Nicholas Edwards MP
House of Commons
London
SW1AA 0AA

17th June 1977

Dear Mrs Granville,
I enclose a copy of a letter I have received from the Ministry of Defence following the representations I made on your behalf but I am afraid this seems to throw no light on your recent encounter.

Yours sincerely,
[signed] Nicholas Edwards

The enclosed letter read:

Ministry of Defence
Main Building
Whitehall
London SW1

Parliamentary Under Secretary of State
for Defence for the Royal Air Force
AF/JW   199/77   15th June 1977

Dear Nicholas,
My department have investigated the report about an Unidentified Flying Object which you referred to me on 17th May on behalf of Mrs Rose Granville of the Haven

Fort Hotel. I regret to say however that although a RAF officer has visited Mrs Granville we are unable to offer any further information. It is true that the Royal Observer Corps have a post in the adjoining field but there is no evidence that their activities could have seemed unusual in any way and we have no record of any other unusual activity in the area.

I am sorry I cannot be more helpful.

Yours sincerely,
[signed] James Wellbeloved

The situation was a contradictory one. The RAF had obviously taken the incident very seriously, evidenced by their sending a very high-ranking officer to investigate it. His arrival without any other witnesses suggested an element of secrecy, emphasized by his request to the witness to keep the incident undisclosed.

The letter by James Wellbeloved, Parliamentary Under Secretary of State for Defence for the Royal Air Force, stated clearly that they could offer no additional knowledge of the incident in particular but implied that they might know a lot more about the situation than he was allowed to say. Nicholas Edwards MP had sincerely and earnestly tried to extract information on the subject and put Rose's mind at rest, but he was obviously not being told any more about it than the Granvilles knew already.

Also there were other sightings, one by an ex-RAF pilot who had watched about half a dozen UFOs flying in formation over Solva, and one by Mr Peter Burford of Glasfryn, St Clears, who recalls: 'My wife first saw a thin orange-red light on the horizon. It seemed to be pulsating, but for two minutes remained quite stationary.'

The witness had watched it for some twenty minutes before it left its position and moved towards Carmarthen.

Mr Burford tried ringing Carmarthen police and they suggested RAF Brawdy, so he telephoned them.

'The officer on duty asked me to describe what I had seen, remembered Mr Burford. 'When I told him, he said it sounded like one of the UFOs that had been sighted in the Ferryside area recently.

'I would like to feel that what I saw was just a light from a helicopter but I am perfectly sure in my mind that it was something more than that,' Mr Burford added.

Inquiries to the Ministry of Defence in London proved unhelpful to the point of being farcical. They relied upon the Fylingdales Radar Base on the Yorkshire moors for information on ICBMs and satellites from which they were sufficiently satisfied that Britain's defence network could not be penetrated.

Fylingdales has a log of the 10,638 manmade satellites launched since October 1957 when the Russians put up Sputnik I.

A Ministry spokesman added: 'At the moment there are 944 operating pay loads in earth orbit with 56 space probes heading for distant planets and other destinations. We even know of all the satellite debris. We would know pretty quickly if any satellite was infringing United Kingdom air space either through malfunction or deliberately.'

The Ministry spokesman failed to mention what the procedure was if an object was present which was not one of the 10,638 manmade satellites and he stated that the Ministry of Defence was only interested in unexplained phenomena when they were near military bases. He quipped, 'We don't chase witches on broomsticks all over Britain.'

Apparently UFO reports were treated on a local basis by respective air stations and I suspected that any unconventional report finding its way through to Whitehall fell somewhat on deaf ears. The ultimate weapon held by the Ministry against the UFO was simply to file it. When pressed on this point a military spokesman later said, 'The Ministry does not dismiss the possibility that intelligent life can exist in outer space. In the period 1967 to 1972 there were 1,631 flying objects reported. Of these, 203 were satellites and debris, 108 were balloons, 170 were stars, 121 were cloud formations, 750 were aircraft and 106 were flares. Of the remainder there is insufficient evidence to explain them away. They are unexplained sightings.'

This outright admission meant that 173 UFO sightings had remained a complete mystery to the Ministry men.

The spokesman continued, 'In Britain there are two clerks working for the Ministry whose responsibility it is to investigate UFO sightings. These clerks are in a position to call in experts if necessary.'

Asked what the position was relating to messages from outer space, the answer again bordered on the ridiculous. The Ministry spokesman stated, 'Any messages transmitted from outer space are the responsibility of the BBC or the Post Office. It is their responsibility to track down illegal broadcasts.'

The Ministry of Defence's attitude in London towards UFOs as 'witches on broomsticks' was in contrast to the American attitude as expressed by President Carter, who had reported a UFO sighting himself in 1973.

President Carter stated, 'I don't laugh at people any more when they say they've seen UFOs, because I've seen one myself. It was the darndest thing I've ever seen. It was big, it was very bright and it changed colours and it was about the size of the moon. We watched it for ten minutes, but none of us could figure out what it was.'

In another statement he described it as 'luminous, not solid, at first bluish, then reddish ... it seemed to move towards us from a distance, stopped, then moved partially away.'

Reassuringly he also said, 'One thing's for sure, I'll never make fun of people who say they have seen unidentified objects in the sky!'.

Then in 1976 the President elect stated, 'If I become president, I'll make every piece of information this country has about UFO sightings available to the public and to the scientists. I am convinced that UFOs exist, because I have seen one.'

President Carter's twenty-three-year-old son Jeff, when questioned about his father's sighting, said: 'He knew it couldn't have been an aircraft of any type. Remember, he's a nuclear physicist who served with the Navy.'

Mrs Lilian Carter, the seventy-eight-year-old mother of the President, said that the sighting had made a 'huge impression' on her son.

'Jimmy told me about the sighting several times. He's always been a down-to-earth, no-nonsense boy, and the sighting by him, as far as I'm concerned, is as firm as money in the bank.'

The President's 1973 sighting was confirmed by nineteen other witnesses.

Mr Jack Acuff, Director of the National Investigations Committee on Aerial Phenomena, commenting on the President's statement, said: 'Material on UFOs is locked up in the National Archives that has never been made public. If a President were to have it released it would be exciting news to the scientific community, and of inestimable benefit to the public.'

It is a pity since Carter's election to President that he has not been able officially to release more information on UFOs up to the present time. The subject remains classified under order 'JANAP No 2000–2' (Joint Army-Navy-Air Force procedure order), Air Force order AFR 200–2, 80–17, JANAP 146, and NASA KIM–8610. However, there have been a number of interesting leaks. These have occurred not only through NASA but also through the military services, and although one has no direct evidence of it there does seem to be an easing of the restriction on this type of information. At present the CIA is being sued under the Freedom of Information Act for continuing to withhold information on UFOs. This particular legal action is not likely to get anywhere as the CIA are claiming that the information lies outside the jurisdiction of the courts. But the very admission that there is information is significant, and the fact that a member of the general public should be able to tackle them on this point is highly interesting. Certainly the CIA's wings have been considerably clipped since the Watergate affair.

In the United Kingdom UFOs are apparently investigated by a Ministry of Defence department enigmatically called 'F4'. Despite the subject being played down in statements by the Ministry of Defence and also in answers to questions placed by MPs in writing and in the Houses of Parliament, the Ministry would still like people to report their observations. They have requested: 'If people do believe they have seen something, we would be grateful if they would send a report to the Ministry of Defence.'

It is definitely known that the MOD do have many reports on their files, most of which have never been released to the general public. For example, one letter in my records reads:

I am an ex-RAF (Squadron Leader) Pilot and after the war was a flying instructor; the incident I remember happened at Carlisle in 1947. Giving a pupil instructions on night landings using a power long approach method, we both noticed that after turning from base leg on to final and aligning the aircraft with the flare path there appeared a hovering object in front of us about 100 to 150 ft lower than us. It was giving off a blue-white appearance, shaped like a child's metal spinning top, with an astrodome sited on its peak, a span of approximately 40 ft. I increased speed to attempt overtaking for a closer look, but when within approximately 100 yards, and we were level at about 150 ft above ground, it moved away at such a speed I knew I had no hope of getting closer.

As I returned to straight and level prior to climbing to complete another circuit I had to fly through the space that had been occupied by this craft. It felt that I had flown through the slipstream of another plane, so we knew that something had disturbed the air to create this turbulence.

The flare-path controller thought it was a light reflection and dismissed what we had seen.

End of incident!

Another near-miss report came from C. A. S. Davey and was as follows:

July 28th, 1973, 11 p.m., Newton Abbot – Clear night, full moon – I was watching an airliner flying over Newton Abbot. Then all of a sudden my friend said to me to look at this other thing and to my surprise it was, as I could make out, a UFO. It was a red disc shape which came across the path of the plane and took the same flight path for a few seconds, then the red disc veered slightly and so did the plane in the same direction. As soon as the plane did this the red disc flew off in the direction of Teignmouth at what I can only describe as incredible speed. If the airliner was travelling at 600 mph then I estimate that the red disc had to be travelling at 2,000 mph plus, when it flew off.

This incident occurred on the A25 airlane in proximity to the junction of flight path DR8 north of Dawlish beacon.

It has been noticed that, after the late 1950s, UFOs have appeared to carry a number of what seem to be navigation lights which are a copy of the colours in use by commercial aircraft. They usually flash and are red, green and orange, also sometimes blue or yellow, but nearly always a constant red light is displayed. Continuous white lights are also common, rather like landing lights and I have myself seen this on a craft that was of no earthly origin.

My sighting occurred on 30 June 1976 at Warminster. Gliding in from the north at an altitude no higher than 8,000 ft had come a circular craft carrying clearly defined lights. Its speed was quite slow, approximately 250 knots and it undulated slightly in its flight path. No flashing anti-

73

collision lights could be detected but through 10×50 glasses four white lights could be seen arranged in a square on the underside with a fifth white light in the centre of the square, along with a steady red light ahead and below the central white light. All of these illuminations were constant points and clearly visible.

I have seen before many military aircraft and I was certain this craft was not of War Department origin.

Its body was metal grey, sharply outlined in the evening light. No sound could be heard and as it flew over the copse at Cradle Hill, some quarter of a mile west, it banked from north to west and I could clearly see that there were no wings or aerofoils on the fuselage. Neither could any windows be observed, or exhaust. A very faint sound like that of an electric turbine was detected by other witnesses present, who included an engineer from the British Aircraft Corporation; but it in no way sounded like a jet engine.

Later in the evening, high up in the star-spangled sky, over the British Army School of Infantry we had also observed some inexplicable, bright flashing lights. They were very brilliant and of a high colour temperature, towards 5,000°K. One had the impression that some sort of directional flash gun was being used, as the flashes were all of a very short duration, maybe only one thousandth of a second. But they came from a small area in the sky and did not occur in a straight line, neither was any aircraft noise audible before or afterwards and whatever was making the flashing, the beam of light from it was definitely directed downwards and did not originate from the ground. The change of position of the point of origin of the flashes was so fast that the distance could not possibly have been traversed by an aircraft or helicopter and the lights were not moving in a regular orbital path, hence could not have been from a satellite. They definitely were not lightning or any form of meteorite.

The following day, at 4 a.m. and 4.10 a.m. a glowing

golden disc was also seen in the vicinity, only 100 ft off the ground.

I myself had also seen a golden-coloured circular object before, this time near Dartmoor. The object appeared to be travelling at no higher than 3,000 ft, was perfectly silent and seemed to be rotating. When signalled by a 150-watt mercury quartz ultraviolet lamp, it suddenly increased in brilliance, changed course by 30° and climbed away until it could no longer be seen in the starlit sky. There was nothing definite to indicate that this was a direct response to the display of the ultraviolet lamp; however, I can only state that the object was directly overhead when the light was kindled. The UFO's manoeuvre was instantaneous and for all the world looked to me like a high-speed evasive procedure away from our position, gaining both air speed and height combined with a change of heading.

Despite the vast number of inexplicable events occurring particularly around military installations and the apparent surveying of the Anglo-American and NATO installations in the United Kingdom, a Ministry of Defence spokesman was adamant: 'None of the observations reported has proved a threat to the safety of the United Kingdom.'

The statement may well be completely true, but can we allow ourselves this degree of apathy? Indeed such a sentiment could only be truly expressed from one of two points of view: either a complete, blind denial, positively a mental block that the objects do not exist; or alternatively, such an intimate knowledge of their policies and motives that the government accepts them as being of peaceful intent.

Either way the general public needs to know.

But let us for the moment leave aside the contradictory statements of government spokesmen and turn to the situation as it was developing in West Wales. The Granville family had proved of inestimable value to the progress of UFO investigations. By their persistence they had drawn the government out into a definite if somewhat divided position and Mrs Granville had also provided details of a number of extremely interesting occurrences. Before we examine them as a complete picture, let us continue with those events that followed the ones we have already described.

The Granvilles are of unquestionable respectability. They shunned publicity of the events that occurred and they feared the effect it would have on their hard-won business. They own a considerable acreage of land in the key areas of the 'Welsh Triangle' and it was on their land that many of these strange craft were repeatedly landing. Rose, her daughter Francine and her husband Hayden continued to see the strange discs, mostly at night, moving in close proximity to the cliffs which encircle St Brides Bay.

Quite often UFOs would circle the hotel and then move off in the direction of Ripperston Farm and the islands known as Stack Rocks owned by the Granvilles. The family remained apprehensive, but they felt that they had done what they could and to date no harm had come to them. Perhaps their strange intruders were benign after all. Of one thing Mrs Granville was absolutely certain:

'I am sure they are searching for something – something underground.'

She had no idea what it could be, but she asked me to investigate the matter as fully as I could, including historical records and the possibility of some mining connection. To this end she provided me with as much detailed relevant information as she could.

The monolithic slab of stone in her grounds, said to cover the grave of a prehistoric chieftain, did not seem to give us any further clues, but a discussion of the more recent history and architecture of the Haven Fort Hotel turned up trumps. Apparently, subsequent to its purely military role, the fortress had been used as a temporary prison for smugglers. The excise men had kept them captive there before transferring them for trial. Indeed the fortress had something of a history.

A fascinating fact emerged. Directly underneath the north

wing and the disused cottage over which the UFO had hovered and burnt the roof, there was a tunnel. When Mrs Granville bought the hotel, the tunnel was still open and in a usable condition. It linked the beach, some many hundreds of yards below, and travelled up a natural cave and fissure, then it had been excavated up to the castle. Thus it formed a complete underground passageway from the fortress cellars to the shoreline below.

Unfortunately one of the conditions of her insurers was that this tunnel had to be blocked, as it was considered a security risk and a likely weak point where thieves could enter unobserved. So the tunnel had been walled up at both ends and the cellars into which it led were sealed off; hence it was no longer available for internal inspection without a considerable amount of demolition and disruption to the existing floors. However, inside the sealing walls the tunnel remained intact, complete and dry.

So we had an interesting common denominator. Some intense radiation had been directed at her cottage roof which was in proximity to the tunnel. Similarly the near-landing that she had observed in her rear field had been beside a Royal Observer Corps nuclear fall-out shelter, which is also a completely underground installation. The beings who had emerged from the strange aerial craft had appeared to be searching, and possibly placing some small equipment or scanning device on the ground.

Why were the giants so interested in underground cavities? Was there possibly even a remote connection between the craft landing on Ripperston Farm, again directly over an underground water system? Then there had been the UFO landing near the sewerage facility close to the Broad Haven Primary School, a plant which would also have underground lines.

We set to work on the new inquiry immediately, sensing that in this direction perhaps might lie the key which connected all of the apparently unrelated items of information. Our search was moving not only outwards and upwards but also downwards, relative to the surface of the earth.

Our first items of extra data proved inconclusive. Sharon Robbins had reported sighting an unidentified flying object on Sunday 15 May 1977 at midnight.

'As I was driving home I could see a very bright white light high up in the sky which looked like a spotlight. It seemed to be directly above a neighbouring bungalow, but as I drove farther down the lane it became obvious that this wasn't so. The lane curves to a dead end, and there is a field with a sloping hill at the end of the lane. This light was coming from the top of the brow of the hill, on the righthand side. It was very slowly moving to the left. It was like a large ball of bright white "fire", which had a very deep orange smaller circular light at the tail of it. This orange light only lasted for a few seconds, and then vanished, leaving this large ball of white. This hovered across the brow of the hill ever so close to the ground. Very slowly it would rise up, then lower itself again. Twice it looked as if it had landed.

'After the landing this large white light floated across the width of the field, staying at the top – the field being about an acre. It is hard to say how big the ball of white was. To me it seemed about the size of the moon – obviously it wasn't the moon. When it reached the other side, which is still within eyesight, it vanished. The light didn't fade at all, it just disappeared, like the orange light. The whole thing lasted for about five minutes.

'On Monday 16th I went to the spot where it appeared to have been and the grass was flattened in two circular shapes, only the outline or ring of the circles, though. One was much larger than the other and I don't think it could have been made by anything else. The stones around the outskirts of these circles are all scratched in the same direction. The largest diameter of the impression in the ground was about 8 feet.'

Three days later, on 18 May 1977, a couple had watched a UFO hover over a house and then land in a nearby field. Examination of the ground revealed flattened grass and a small hole in the soil but no more information was available; of more significance was a report dated 4 August 1977. A mother and her thirteen-year-old daughter who did not wish to be named, had witnessed an intense amount of aerial activity by twenty or more UFOs manoeuvring in such a fantastic fashion that they could not possibly have been manmade aircraft.

They first noticed five bright lights hovering in the sky above Milford Haven. Suddenly one of the lights moved away seawards. When out over the coast it had stopped and from it had emerged three smaller lights. The new UFOs then flew all over the area, up and down the Haven, before returning to their parent craft where they were picked up again and it rejoined the main group stationary over the town. Then three of the other craft flew out to sea at different points and discharged more lights. These came back inland as a formation of red, green and silver discs totalling nine objects in all.

The performance, which continued for over two hours, included a formation of six UFOs flying low up the Haven at a speed faster than jet aircraft.

The witnesses were describing something that had been seen on various occasions in other parts of the world: some kind of parent or mother craft discharging smaller scouts, possibly remotely controlled, which were surveying in a methodical search pattern. Apparently this phenomenon had been witnessed by other people on different days. Whatever the UFOs were looking for, they were making a pretty intensive effort to find it.

One would imagine that all of these aerial goings-on would be clearly recorded on the local RAF radar, but when the query was raised the answer had always been that on that particular occasion the RAF were not flying and the radar had been switched off. It seemed a strange coincidence that UFOs could time their activity such that they had exclusive use of the air space over Pembrokeshire.

4

Booms – Seismic or Supersonic

During my conversations with the Granville family and leading on from Rose's speculation that her encounters were something to do with possible underground activity, another subject had come to light. The press had clichéd it, 'The Riddle of the Bumps'. The strange mystery had received considerable media coverage in November and December of 1976, but no solution had been found.

The 'bumps' constituted a series of regular and violent vibrations that had been shaking the West Country, in particular areas along the Bristol Channel, during the latter half of 1976, throughout 1977 and on up to the present time.

The first person to complain about them officially was county council engineer George Lawrence of North Petherton. He sought the assistance of aeronautical experts from Bristol University and inquiries were made by the local police. An appeal was launched for as much information as possible and thousands of letters flooded in from residents all over the area complaining of the noise.

Dick Challen, a civilian police switchboard operator, heard the noise regularly around 9.00 every evening.

He said: 'They make the windows rattle and at the same time as I first started to hear the bangs, cracks began to appear in the plaster.' He described a heavy bump, followed thirty seconds later by three bumps in quick succession.

Another report came from Yeovilton Naval Air Station nearly twenty miles away. Public Relations Lieutenant Clifford Humphreys said: 'I was sitting in the kitchen of my home and the whole house resonated. It was a double thump, then a break of fifteen seconds or so, then a second double thump.'

Reports flooded in day after day. People reported strange

rumblings followed a minute or two later by further explosions and strong vibrations. They occurred usually around 9 o'clock in the evening but sometimes had been heard at 6.20 p.m., 10.20 p.m. and at 12.50 midday.

Dr James Fleming of Wookey Wells said: 'It was a loud bang and the house shook then it was followed by a smaller bang.'

Mr Alex Kirley of Downend said: 'I was outside the house at the time and distinctly heard three heavy bumps just like distant gunfire,' and Mrs Marion Perry of Middle Leigh stated: 'This was the worst it has been. The windows shook and the house rattled.'

Not only was people's property being shaken to the roots and in some cases slightly damaged but gamekeepers also became alarmed. Apparently the noise was disturbing roosting pheasants, reared at the county council's farm institute in Cannington. Sidney Cable said that the birds became restless about fifteen seconds before the boom.

Dr Robert Adams, one of the Bristol University researchers working on the mystery, said: 'They seem to hear low-frequency sounds which occur just before the boom that is audible to us. Just because many of the sounds are outside human range, it does not mean they are inaudible to animals, and they are probably more sensitive to low-frequency noise than we are. I have a pretty strong suspicion as to what is causing it but I am not prepared to say until we have worked this thing out scientifically; but it is certainly not caused by the conventional over-flying of supersonic aircraft.'

Thomas Lawson, Reader in Industrial Aerodynamics at Bristol University, also heard the sounds and stated: 'They could not have been made by a supersonic aircraft because of the long gap between them. I have heard nothing like it before. It sounded rather like thunder, yet it was not thunder. At the moment I just cannot explain what causes the bangs, and I would like to go into it a lot further.'

A spokesman for the Global Seismology Unit of the

Institute of Geological Sciences in Edinburgh speculated: 'The fact that the noises occur at the same time every night leads one to believe that they are manmade.'

Neither could the Ministry of Defence be of any help. A spokesman said: 'We certainly have no trace of any military aircraft activity that could explain it, and in any case this is nothing like a sonic boom. They tend to be more of a sharp report, and this is a long rumbling sound.'

The experts from Bristol University set up mechanical recording equipment and oscilloscopes to register the sound, but could find no explanation from the wave pattern to identify its origin.

Dr Adams said: 'I have no theories about the bang at all except that it was not caused by an aircraft.'

The phenomena continued, and fire crew at Lulsgate airport reported a shockwave at 9.14 p.m. on 18 November 1976. Dave Matthews, a thirty-four-year-old fireman, recalls, 'The complete place shook for several minutes; it sounded like someone was running on top of the roof.'

By this time Concorde was the favourite scapegoat explanation for the strange vibrations, but the tremors continued regularly even on nights and at times when no Concordes of either British Airways or Air France were in the air, or scheduled to be anywhere near the area of the reports. A civil aviation authority expert on sonic booms stated: 'It seems most unlikely that the sonic booms of the Air France Concorde could be heard up the Bristol Channel. The usual carpet for hearing sonic booms is about twenty miles. At thirty miles the sound has disappeared or very nearly so. Yet this noise is being heard at far greater distances.'

On several occasions a strange orange glow had been seen in the sky after the boom had occurred, in one case taking the form of a fireball that hurtled at high speed across the sky before vanishing. One man from Coombe Down said, 'I thought I was going round the bend', after having witnessed the phenomenon. Meanwhile the coincidence of

UFO activity on dates and in locations not too distant from the area of the noises continued to occur. On 19 November 1976, Brian Jones of Llanelli had witnessed a frightening 'fireball' emitting sparks over the village of Llanerch, while other reports came in from Cwmbran. Mr Kevin Miely, a security officer, saw a weird object while he was patrolling a building site.

He stated: 'It was a clear night and all the stars were out. I was just doing the rounds when I noticed this star-like thing hovering over the mountain. It was not like any of the other stars – a lot bigger in fact – and it was flashing red, green and white. There was an eerie presence about it – as if it was watching over Cwmbran. I kept an eye on it while I walked the site and I noticed that very slowly it was descending.'

When it disappeared he recalls: 'I did not see it again – in fact I did not want to see it. It made me feel uncomfortable and I confess that in my type of job you need to have a firm backbone.'

It was also observed by Glynn Burn and his girlfriend from Tycoch: 'It appeared to be over Henllys. There was a strange glow from it and it looked as though it was flashing orange and white. It seemed to have a tail stretching from it but at that stage it did not look as though it was moving.' Mr Burn said that the object disappeared eventually towards the Pontypool area. A similar object was also sighted by David Awcock, a production foreman at Panteg steelworks.

The pattern that emerged out of the numerous reports of both sounds and sightings seemed to indicate that the infamous 'bumps' or 'booms' were definitely manmade, but the association of UFO sightings occurring with them shortly afterwards indicated the possibility of some kind of surveillance being undertaken on what had caused the strange vibrations. There was considerable disagreement as to whether the sounds originated in the air, the upper stratosphere or from underground tremors.

I myself witnessed the phenomena on numerous occasions whilst staying in Wales, and indeed the shockwaves on occasion were very severe. In fact the first time the shock occurred I instinctively ran to the door, associating it with some form of minor earthquake. I had felt this sort of thing before during an earth tremor when I was in Italy; similarly I had also on other occasions heard numerous sonic booms and this sound did not resemble that very characteristic bang but a vibration much lower. In fact one was very aware of 'feeling' the sound as well as hearing it. It was noticeable that often one was first aware of it by the rattling of loose glass or the jangling of objects which in turn made a sound, rather than hearing the audible frequency first. The feeling was that the sound originated from some source of tremendous power deeply removed, possibly underground, with the frequency spreading out over a very wide area. The numerous 'echoes' suggested geological reflections, or even a physically transmitted sound followed by an airborne sound some short time afterwards.

Sound in air travels at 1,100 feet per second, but in other mediums such as water and different types of rock it travels at different speeds. Hence it is possible that a single explosion may be heard more than once by virtue of the sound's passage through different mediums of substance, air, ground or water accordingly. This possibly was the case where the ultrasonic frequencies were sensed by the animals first, followed by an audible signal which could be heard by the witnesses.

All in all, however, very little was known about the mystery and eventually it was written off to Concorde. This quietened the unrest, without giving a definite explanation. There remained the possibility that the actual cause of the vibration was some secret operation, hence the powers-that-be who did know what was causing it did not find themselves in a position to reveal all.

Another thing seemed indicated by the series of reports. When the vibrations had begun they had done so at a more variable range of times than later in the year of 1977. But as the public became more interested in them they seem to have been synchronized with the flights of Concorde both to and from London Heathrow airport and Charles de Gaulle airport, Paris. This would have made an excellent cover for any tremors that were felt, and hence there might even have been the case where witnesses were hearing two vibrations from independent sources: the one unexplained, and the other genuinely from Concorde. It seemed likely that the supersonic airliner in most cases had been responsible only for the lesser, quieter sound, and this would explain the very long delays sometimes observed between the different vibrations, ranging from fifteen seconds to two minutes.

Was some government agency or powerful organization conducting some clandestine tunnelling under the Atlantic Ocean? Were underground explosions or tests being masked by a cover explanation so that complaints could be written off to the controversial Anglo-French supersonic jet airliner?

More clues came from witnesses specifically in the 'Welsh Triangle' area. Pauline Coombs, in one of her statements relating the strange things she had observed in St Brides Bay, made the startling comment: 'One day I saw the sea shake.' She went on to explain that she was not referring to ordinary waves on the water but vibration radiating outwards from a point in the bay similar to what one might observe from an underwater explosion or a seismic shockwave. Certainly the phenomenon seemed to be confined to an area within reasonable range of Pembrokeshire, including South Wales, North Devon and North Somerset, all bordering or near to the Bristol Channel and the Atlantic.

If it was underneath the sea, it must have been of considerable power and buried in the deep to produce this range of vibration. True, there was a supersonic military airlane near to the scene of the water vibrations, also various bombing ranges, missile sites and tank ranges; but the phenomenon to which we are referring had displayed a type of frequency and a degree of penetration such that one could not dismiss it with an 'off pat' conventional explanation.

There remained the remote possibility that some extra-terrestrial intelligence was engineering a subterranean mining operation which was causing the strange sounds, but this was unlikely because of their distinct regularity. Constant time patterns had never been noticed before in UFO phenomena and they were not likely to arise now. Therefore the origin of the sounds lay strictly in the camp of manmade phenomena. The purpose and origin we had not yet discovered, so it remained another unknown; but it fitted into the jigsaw somewhere and I felt sure the strange 'bumps' were a significant clue to the enigmatic 'Welsh Triangle'.

5

Caves, Candles and Archives

Pursuing our search for more background information into special characteristics of the 'Welsh Triangle' we spent several days digging through records at the local Haverford-west public library. The results were interesting and brought out the possibility of other factors affecting the mystery. We first consulted the largest available maps they had of the area: a series of interconnecting 6-in to 1-mile Ordnance Survey maps first produced in 1874 but revised in 1906. These showed us that the principal events had occurred in the area of latitude 51° 40 minutes N and longitude 5° 8 minutes W, directly opposite Stack Rocks and near to Ripperston Farm which we found had an altitude of 149 ft above sea level.

Of particular interest in our geological review we found

that the entire coastline of St Brides Bay is riddled with deeply penetrating sea caves, some of them large caverns several hundred yards long; and we also learnt that these connected with underground fissures to other caverns that spread out underneath the surrounding villages and the air station at RAF Brawdy.

According to the 1906 map, the area contained various disused mine workings, long since abandoned due to the uneconomic yield of the measures being worked. The area around Ripperston Farm contained numerous natural springs and a proliferation of prehistoric monuments. These included an extensive long barrow at Talbenny, orientated towards the coast and directly in line with Stack Rocks. Ripperston Farm itself was built on the site of another long barrow, whose physical presence is no longer visible. Along the coast were remnants of many Celtic raths, and at other locations near to the significant area were forts, earthworks, mottes, burial chambers and some standing stones, most of them dating from the period of the 'Windmill Hill and Beaker peoples' of prehistoric Britain.

Neolithic Man had certainly been pretty busy in this part of the world and as in other areas such as Cornwall, Devon, Wessex and the Western Isles of Scotland his monuments, mysterious and impressive, stand in silent testimony to a great age gone by.

In more recent times, during the grand old days of smuggling, the Pembrokeshire coast had a colourful history. It had proved the excise man's nightmare and the 'ferryman's' paradise with its coves, caves and islands. Indeed some of the names of the secluded and remote inlets along the coast evidenced this very strong connection: Brandy Bay, Dutch Gin, Silver, and Foxes' Holes. Pirates had also established bases on various islands, numerous off the coast, from which they had raided shipping heading out of Milford Haven. Much of their plunder still remained hidden and buried in the caves or on offshore islands, fair game for modern-day treasure hunters equipped with metal detectors. It was not uncommon for remains of gin stills to be found hidden in underground retreats or buried in the sand. Inside the caves had been found candles, jars and other artifacts from that romantic period. More of interest to us than these was a legend which stated that there was a smugglers' tunnel which ran from Stack Rocks underground to a hidden exit somewhere on the mainland, but nobody knew exactly where this was and the location was open to speculation. However, it seemed that many of these old tunnels were still in good order as they had been excavated through soft but solid rock and had not required pit props; therefore they would be likely to survive history and would not decay as in a structure of a more artificial nature. Of course many of them had employed natural fissures and caverns in the geologically twisted and faulted strata.

Another very noticeable characteristic of the 'Triangle' was a large number of disused wartime aerodromes, including one at South Hill in proximity to Ripperston Farm. Many of these had been either ploughed up or just left to decay into a desolate landscape of rusting and smashed concrete buildings, but much of the area was still under the MOD administration and remained closed to the general public.

One incredible item of information which could be more significant than at first glance was that off Newgale Sands, near Brawdy Air Station, there lies hidden below the waters of the Atlantic Ocean a petrified forest of truncated tree stumps. These are shown on the Ordnance Survey map of 1874 and had been testified to by numerous residents who, at periods of extremely low tidal water, had seen those trees closest to the shoreline sticking up out of the water. Exactly from which period they dated was not clear. However, they irrefutably stated by their presence that St Brides Bay at one time in the distant past had been dry land and many of the islands, now only clumps of desolate rock inhabited by seabirds, had been the summit of hills looking over perhaps a lush and green countryside. The bay itself apparently was relatively shallow and although it afforded shelter for some ships it was not deep enough in parts to house very large vessels.

There is a legend which associates the British Isles as being at one time a territorial province on the eastern perimeter of that mythical and much speculated continent of Atlantis. According to the legend, the British Isles were known as the 'Isles of the Blest', and during the final days of the island continent of Poseidon, when that land was breaking up due to some kind of seismic activity, numerous refugees of that supposed early culture fled to the east, bringing their knowledge to western Britain. Could this early influx have given rise to the many and huge constructions of mysterious and largely inexplicable earthworks and mounds, and to works of megalithic engineering?

Certainly the sea level or the land level has changed in St Brides Bay, causing vast areas of countryside to disappear under the waves of the relentless ocean. Also, local scuba divers have informed me that the majority of St Brides Bay is a flat underwater desert of golden sand, affording excellent visibility and clear water, while in the vicinity of the islands and rocks there is good underwater hunting for crabs, lobsters and crayfish.

Was there some special significance in the possibly Atlantean connection of the area which encouraged the UFOs to centre their activity in this ancient land of western Wales? Were they even utilizing or revitalizing some ancient facility or power source?

In recent years much intensive research has been done on the deeper significance of this prehistoric period of gigantic building in earth and stone. One of the amazing facts that has emerged is that the monuments individually cannot be treated in isolation. For it is now indicated and claimed by some writers that many of the monuments in different parts of the British Isles form gigantic zodiacs and star maps of the heavens. Examples of these are the Glastonbury Zodiac in Somerset which is said to be some ten miles in diameter; and recent research on the ancient kingdom of Wessex has shown that the long barrows of the counties of Berkshire, Cornwall, Devon, Dorset, Gloucestershire, Oxfordshire, Somerset, South Wales and Wiltshire form a single gigantic star map of the heavens, with individual long barrows marking stars and greater earthworks such as hill forts marking galaxies and nebulae. How this vast network of monuments was laid out with such precision is difficult to imagine without supposing some ability in aerial surveying or methods of triangulation more accurate than we give this ancient people credit for.

The discovery of the alignment of these monuments has led to the publication of numerous works on the subject of 'leys'. Originating from the research of Thom and Watkins who first discovered the ancient straight tracks, it has now been found that many of the monuments line up systematically across the country, covering hundreds of miles and forming geometrical patterns which have not yet been fully understood. However, the common figures which emerge are predominantly triangles. The constructions show a determination and resourcefulness on the part of this culture which must have extended over a period of hundreds or even thousands of years. It seems that whatever was undertaken by the ancient constructors was done for purposes other than those for which they are normally recognized, and much of what they built incorporated a hidden esoteric meaning based on the structure of the cosmos.

Over 4,000 years ago a group of people entered the British Isles with a profound knowledge of astronomy. They spread across the British Isles an array of monuments, burial mounds and other landmarks, the true significance of which up to the present century has somehow escaped detection, although their secret was buried in legend. Within the last few decades these monumental works of antiquity have been deciphered and have caused us to sit back and ponder anew concerning the technology of our forebears.

Research into the layout of the long barrows has shown that they are more than just burial mounds. Much of what the ancients built was intended to have a dual meaning and this is as true for Stonehenge as it is for the Great Pyramid at Giza.

The long barrows, wedge-shaped burial mounds, have always been an enigma. Prehistorians state that they were clearly built for the interment of large numbers of corpses, sometimes totalling hundreds, and remained in use for up to a century, being opened periodically for further burials. In fact there is little evidence for this, and no long barrows to my knowledge have ever produced that many corpses when excavated. It is also stated that barrows were built for chieftains and the eminent members of society, but this also is not always borne out as many of the bones found during archaeological inspection of the sites were at relatively shallow depths and seem to have been added to the structure many years after their completion, rather than being connected with its original purpose.

The long barrows were built in the Neolithic period somewhere around 3,000 BC, before the Bronze Age and after the Palaeolithic. People of the Windmill Hill culture erected these giant burial mounds, of which long barrows are the oldest of the various types. Later types are: bowl, bell, disc, pond and saucer barrows, all of which are in the category of round barrows and are names derived from the shape of their construction, together with the ancient white horses.

Studies of the apparently haphazard locations of the monuments have revealed the incredible fact that the long barrows are laid out in familiar patterns, for all of them form with amazing precision a large number of the constellations of the northern sky and are moreover placed in the correct positions on the ecliptic.

The star field is spread out over many hundreds of square miles of open countryside and includes the constellations of Boötes, Pegasus, Cassiopeia, Ursa Minor, Ursa Major,

Perseus, Taurus, Capricorn, and so on, depicted with uncanny accuracy.

According to conventional archaeological thinking the majority of these monuments have only a religious significance, being either graves, avenues of stones for ceremonial occasions or meeting-places of pagan importance. However, it has been shown by such scholars as Prof. Gerald Hawkins that many of the monuments have a much deeper astrological and astronomical significance. In his book *Stonehenge Decoded* (1966), Hawkins demonstrates that Stonehenge was used not just as a temple but as an astronomical computer and yearly calendar giving precise information on the position of the moon and sun even to the extent of predicting eclipses. This same principle of stone circles being directly connected to a study of the stars can clearly be shown at many other sites throughout the United Kingdom, making the findings at Stonehenge not peculiar to that one great ancient monument but a fine example of a much wider art.

Indeed the ancients' knowledge of the stars is amazing and indications have come from various researches that they had available to them information on distant stars and stellar bodies which we ourselves have only discovered in recent years with the use of high magnitude telescopes and twentieth-century technology. How the ancient people acquired their knowledge when allegedly they had hardly discovered the wheel gives rise to a growing disquiet that our assessment of their intellectual achievements is grossly inaccurate.

Apart from their amazing placement, geographical relationship and siting angles to star positions, it has also been shown recently that many of the monuments have unusual magnetic characteristics. In one experiment it was shown that the magnetic field of the earth increased considerably from the base of one menhir to its summit, and possibly even a spiral magnetic effect was caused. How this was achieved is difficult to say, but the proximity of underground running water seemed to figure in the mechanism; and this characteristic of an increased magnetic field and special magnetic patterns applies not just to one but to a very large number of these ancient Celtic religious sites. The findings lend weight to various claims by people in the past that the stones have special qualities influencing fertility, healing and even the capacity of music. It does seem that at certain times of astrological alignment some unknown and special effects do occur at these locations. Some people claim that they have had electric shocks from the stones and even that they have heard a curious humming noise.

There is a growing feeling among people who have studied this particular aspect of the subject that the 'ley' system is more than just a convenient alignment of landmarks for crossing the countryside; and that the construction of the megaliths was orientated more towards the utilization of some natural and powerful force which is freely available in the earth and originates possibly in cosmic rays or from the influences of stars and planets.

Stonehenge is now recognized as a sophisticated observatory, but was it once a power station in a megalithic 'national grid'?

Scientists know that our ancestors used complex mathematical and geometrical theorems to construct their standing-stone sites. Further research shows that every standing stone in Britain is in a direct line with two or more other prehistoric sites. For example, if you continue a line along the summer solstice at Stonehenge it will pass through the ancient fertility figure of the Cerne Giant in Dorset before reaching the coast at Pucknolle Beacon.

Advocates of the ley lines claim that the old stones show traces of an electromagnetic power. Were they therefore aligned as 'grids' to trap, store or boost some life force known to dwellers on earth long ago? Considering the stones' obvious astronomical significance, it is a fascinating thought that these so-called primitive peoples could have held a lost knowledge of the universe. Indeed many of the old legends and myths brought down to the twentieth century in the cults of witchcraft and magic contain many a truism, often not realized by the twentieth-century practitioners of the art.

Is this another dim memory of a science long forgotten?

It is curious that a large number of Neolithic and pre-Christian monuments are constructed of various forms of rock containing silica and quartz. At Stonehenge, for instance, and at many other ancient sites, the standing stones and lintels are made of sarsen which is a salicified sandstone, while the inner-circle 'blue stones' are known to have come from only one region, the Prescelly Mountains of western Wales.

Sandstone is a rock consisting primarily of quartz sand cemented with silica, which is white or colourless and formed of extremely hard crystalline silicon dioxide (SiO_2). The Great Pyramid, for instance, was primarily constructed from limestone and from granite, a rock containing quartz. It is interesting how many of the principal monuments were constructed of quartz-bearing rock. These include many menhirs, dolmans and standing stones. Noticeably the great serpent temple at Avebury shows the use of sarsen as also the West Kennett Avenue, formed of pairs of lozenge- and rectangular-shaped stones. The Hurlers, Mean Castle, Trencrom, and the Tolvan Stone and the Men-an-tol in Cornwall – the last two having circular holes chipped out of their centres – are all of granite.

The particular significance and characteristic of quartz and its crystals is its piezoelectric quality. Piezoelectricity is the generation of an electric charge in a substance by a mechanical stress. A proportional change in the shape of the substance causes a voltage to occur in the material. The prefix 'piezo' originates from the Greek verb 'to press' and the phenomenon occurs only in material of an electrically polar nature, especially in single crystals of polar symmetry.

Piezoelectricity is a means of converting mechanical

energy into electrical energy or vice versa. It is known that the technique is particularly effective at high frequencies and it is used principally these days in the fields of electroacoustics such as phonograph pickups, and underwater sound signalling and sonar devices. In electronics it is also used in the frequency control of resonant circuits by virtue of its very stable mechanical resonance frequencies of crystal plates, noticeably those cut in specific orientations from quartz crystals of high precision. Many of these quartz-controlled circuits have been important elements in space communication systems used by NASA and the Soviet Union.

These days we create crystals artificially by growing them under special conditions. Present-day crystals are usually created from Rochelle salt and ammonium di-hydrogen phosphate, under conditions of high temperature and pressure. Even quartz crystals can now be produced this way and crystals have been extensively used in radio and television transmission for many years. One of the special characteristics of quartz is the absence of twinning, i.e. the capacity of any particular crystal to be in sympathy only with one which is its exact replica. Thus the possibility arises that if some method of communication was utilizing the stones and crystals employed in these ancient monuments, they could well be finely tuned to others at different locations which had been modified and sculptured to oscillate at identical frequencies, almost an early if effective telegraphic network, or Neolithic 'crystal set'.

The other essential characteristic of quartz-bearing rock is that, in theory, if it were oscillated by sound it should produce an electrical charge, or, correspondingly, if put under alternating electrical stress it should produce a sound and here may be the connection between the chemical constituent of the rocks and the fabled 'singing stones'.

The piezoelectric action of quartz and its silica-containing rocks could also produce some form of power circuitry. It is possible that ancient cultures may have stumbled across this fact or even have been educated in its use by early extraterrestrial mentors. A curious coincidence is that piezoelectric transducers are particularly well matched to the recording and pickup of sounds in water rather than in air, and hydrophonic equipment used for listening to submarine engine noises and the like would also be using this type of material to receive and transmit signals to the listening station. Piezoelectric generators and receivers of sound waves are also used for the input and output of the acoustic delay lines employed in many computers.

Quartz has exceptional chemical and mechanical stability while being unusually elastic. While most materials show decreases in their elastic moduli with an increase in temperature, quartz has the opposite trend, tending to be more elastic as it gets hotter. Another characteristic peculiar to this strange and beautiful stone is that it efficiently allows ultraviolet rays to pass through it uninterrupted, as opposed to the conventional window-pane glass which is UV-opaque; hence many ultraviolet sunlamps employ quartz tubes filled with mercury vapour for the production of their suntanning rays.

It is strangely significant that some symmetrical association has been found between the regular paths of the enigmatic UFOs and the straight tracks of the ancient ley system. Why should these supposedly advanced craft in any way follow paths known and marked by the ancients thousands of years ago? It seems possible from the type of rock used in the construction of the monoliths and from their special magnetic characteristics that the function of the leys and the sites along them could have been to amplify and enhance magnetic lines of force already existent and flowing in the surface of the earth. Such patterns could remain relatively stable and unchanged for long periods of time, and although the effect may be minor, if a craft was using some form of magnetic drive linked in some way to that of the earth's weak magnetic field, any form of enhancement would certainly increase its propulsion capabilities. Whether the ley system is still functioning in its original form or has fallen into disuse is an open question.

6

Big Games and Small People

More information indicating the connection between UFO activity and some underground operation was brought to light by Pauline Coombs when she mentioned that the craft which had landed in her lower field had taken off and moved at a low altitude over the cliffs where it had descended out of her sight towards the shoreline. At this exact location the coastal path and an area of the cliffs had mysteriously cascaded into the sea, causing a minor landslip which restricted access along the coastal path which runs the entire length of the Pembrokeshire coast. This occurrence suggested that possibly the UFO had planted another device in the rockface, or maybe some emission or beam from the craft probing the soil had caused an existing fissure to give way.

More intriguing even than this was the statement by Pauline's husband Billy that the path had been repaired by the Army. Numerous lorries and equipment had arrived, camping in a field near to the landslip and staying for several days, during which time the coastal path was rebuilt; and the whole area had been crawling with military personnel.

Was this purely the Army giving a helping hand or were they more concerned in locating the device or cavity in the cliffs? The location had been directly opposite the islands known as Stack Rocks, over which Rose Granville had seen so much activity and aerial manoeuvring by the elusive

UFOs. Dramatic implications from another sighting indicated mutual interest of the military and the spacecraft in each other, and elevated the scale and scope of the happenings into an international twilight zone of secret activities.

It came to light that the NATO base of RAF Brawdy, situated directly opposite Ripperston Farm and Stack Rocks on the other side of St Brides Bay, was far from being an ordinary installation. Its history was quite normal up to April 1971. Until this time it had been a Royal Naval air station operating two squadrons of the Fleet Air Arm 849 Airborne Early Warning Squadron, 738 Jet Pilot Training Squadron and a large naval air support unit. In 1971 the installation was axed by the Wilson administration on the grounds of defence cuts arising out of the Budget, and all preparation was made for the complete closure of the establishment.

But something happened in 1971 which caused the NATO forces to take UFOs more seriously. The Navy departed completely but new arrangements were made for the Royal Air Force to take over Brawdy. Superficially this was done to appease local residents concerned with harmful effects to the local economy caused by the departure of the military establishment. The station first operated for twelve months with only a skeleton staff of RAF officers continuing its administration.

The role of the RAF at the new Brawdy was supposedly to be one of a training station to familiarize pilots with advanced fighter aircraft and weaponry. A secondary role of weaponry testing was also included in its operational facilities. The curious thing about this new role was that the Pembrokeshire coastline has a notorious weather record. Indeed a pilot at the civilian Haverfordwest aerodrome, recently reopened to serve the Celtic oil industry, stated: 'We have the worst bloody weather in the British Isles. Last week, five out of seven days we were grounded due to weather conditions.'

Ex-Navy pilots from the former Fleet Air Arm station at

Brawdy verified that the weather on this peninsula was atrocious: if it wasn't fog it was wind and rain driving in off the Atlantic. This seemed a very strange place to site a new Royal Air Force training unit which would surely require the best possible conditions, similar to those in East Anglia at the Central Flying School, where the available flying time is enhanced by stable meteorology, unlike that of the blustery Atlantic coast.

The mystery was deepened by the very low-profile arrival of an extensive American contingent whose role seemed unclear and cloaked in secrecy. In the meantime the Brawdy installation had been expanded rather than run down, with the complete clearing of the airfield of all but the most essential personnel and the extending of the runways to facilitate the arrival of any size of aircraft available in the world, including huge American air transporters. Though undertaken without fuss or publicity the works at the base were, I found, common knowledge among local residents, who as in all small communities took a particular interest in strange goings-on. They informed me that the Americans had built an extensive and deep underground facility on a piece of the base that was their exclusive property and to which not even RAF personnel were admitted. On the surface there was very little visible, but apparently the facility was fully equipped to withstand a direct nuclear hit.

This information was of course hearsay, but I had no reason to doubt it and indeed it was not uncommon to other American facilities in other parts of the world. The strange thing was that in this particular instance, rather than publicizing it, which is sometimes the case with United States policy, the whole establishment seemed to prefer to remain in the background.

No American military vehicles were seen in the town or in the surrounding countryside, neither were any uniformed American personnel in evidence. Apparently the slightest infringement by any members of the establishment immediately sent them Stateside, even if they got booked for a parking ticket. I had noticed that I had never seen Americans in numbers greater than two at a time in the town and always in civilian dress. The occasional American plated 'yank tank', as the cars were nicknamed, was glimpsed but never in numbers to be conspicuous.

Exteriorly the American installation looked insignificant enough, rather like a collection of low modern office buildings. The only noticeable feature from outside was the very high degree of security mechanisms surrounding them.

Even the official name of the installation remained something of a mystery. In various statements the base was described as an oceanographic research station, but apparently it fell within the administration of the United States Navy and was headed by a Captain Robert Fellingham. Rather than being staffed by civilians, as one would expect in oceanographic research, its complement was entirely military personnel totalling 600 including their dependants. Most of the former Royal Navy married quarters were now inhabited by Americans. The other strange thing was that on three occasions and by three entirely unrelated people I was told that the Americans had a lot of good geologists there: an interesting piece of information for a base apparently undertaking purely oceanographic research. It was thought that the US installation was a hydrophonic link station, but could there be a connection between the base and other underground activity we were beginning to suspect? The UFOs certainly seemed to be especially interested in the base and its strange function.

Stephen Taylor, a seventeen-year-old youth who lives right on the edge of the NATO installation at Brawdy in the small hamlet of Pen-y-cwm, was witness to an enlightening encounter which occurred on 13 March 1977. He was returning home after escorting his girlfriend to her house when at about 9 o'clock on a fine evening he saw a light in the sky.

He remembers: 'I didn't think much about it', and he dropped in to see some friends and mentioned the strange object.

'They thought I was joking,' he said. He continued his walk home alongside the perimeter fence of the American installation, and recalls: 'A dog came tearing out of the darkness towards me.' He noticed that the lights of a farmhouse that he was accustomed to seeing were no longer visible on the righthand side of him.

He remembers: 'Then I made out a black shape. It looked about 40 ft to 50 ft across. I noticed a dim glow around what seemed to be the underside.'

For one moment he thought the farmer had built a new silo and it was this that was blocking the view of the farmhouse lights, but as he went closer he realized that the farm was obscured by a huge dome-shaped object which had landed in the field and was occupying more than half of it. Within sight of the object was a Ministry of Defence sign stating that no unauthorized person was allowed beyond that point and that the facility came within the meaning of the Official Secrets Act. It was outside this secret installation and in direct proximity to the supposedly innocent oceanographic research station that the UFO had landed.

Stephen leant on the gate, observing the UFO, and lit a cigarette. Maybe it was the light from his match that gave away his position for suddenly he heard a noise like someone stepping on dry leaves and he looked away to his right. Standing near to him was a figure.

'He was like a skinny human and about 6 ft tall,' he recalls.

Stephen was terrified by the appearance of the figure wearing a one-piece protective silver spacesuit and even more so by his facial characteristics, for this other-worldly 'astronaut' was not wearing the visor as described in the other sightings of the giants.

'I noticed high cheekbones, like an old man's, and large eyes like a fish's – round and sort of glazed,' Stephen stated.

The figure had a box-like device over where its mouth would be and a thick dark tube leading from this over its shoulder, exactly the same as the visitor to Ripperston

Farm who watched Billy and Pauline Coombs nearly six weeks later on the evening of 24 April.

Stephen remembers: 'I took a swing at it, and fled. I don't know whether I hit it. I never looked back, but kept on running till I got home.'

In spite of his panic Stephen remembers that the spacesuit was 'transparent but not transparent', and silver-coloured. There was something like a zip fastener which ran from the neck to the waist of the suit and the figure seemed to be wearing some form of breathing apparatus, as in the case of the sighting by Mark Marston who saw a similarly dressed figure on 15 April, one month after Stephen's frightening experience. Also, when Stephen arrived home, he found that his pet Pomeranian dog, normally an affectionate animal, was very upset by some undetermined cause and he recalls, 'Its hair was standing on end. I can't explain it.' However, the dog was back to normal by the following day.

More common denominators now became apparent out of this new report. Stephen's UFO and occupant had been on the very perimeter of the American base at Brawdy. Rather than the 'ufonaut' being interested in Stephen, he seemed more interested in the base, and indeed there was a likelihood that he may have been observing it closely when he was disturbed by the youth returning home.

The UFOs had been systematically surveying the Pembrokeshire coastline in the immediate vicinity of St Brides Bay, also the American facility, and furthermore they had shown a particular interest in underground cavities, as at the Haven Fort Hotel. The American installation also had underground levels. What were the Americans doing in Wales and why were the UFOs so interested in them? We listened further to local residents but did not confront the military directly or ask any questions of the military personnel.

In London a Ministry of Defence spokesman stated: 'We have heard the reports of sightings of unexplained objects in the West Wales area. The people who report these sightings are not nutcases. They are genuinely sincere people genuinely concerned. We investigate every report on this assumption. We do not discount the possibility of intelligent life in outer space.'

The community relations officer at RAF Brawdy, Flight Lieutenant Cohen, stated: 'There have been a flood of these reports. The ground sightings do not, in time or place, fit in with our operations. Neither do the descriptions of spacemen fit with the protecting clothing used by oil refineries in the area. We accept the possibility of life in outer space. But none of our radar units can explain these sightings.'

It was noticeable that the Flight Lieutenant did not deny that radar contact had been made; he stated only that the sightings could not be explained.

The key to the 'Welsh Triangle' I felt was in some way connected with the American activities and we set to work to search for previous press-cuttings that might give some indication of what was going on. The results were contradictory. In one reported incident a local trawler had fished up a thick cable entangled in its trawl nets, and this had later been identified as being of American origin and connected with the oceanographic research base. It had been stated at the time that the Brawdy base was engaged in submarine tracking by ocean surveillance by means of hydrophonic equipment sited somewhere in the near Atlantic and connected to the landbase by cables running out under St Brides Bay. By listening to the engine throb of Russian and other foreign submarines it was possible to identify the name of the vessel and its country of origin precisely by processing the received signals through computers. Brawdy was the only American installation in Wales and apparently was linked with other American installations at Lakenheath and Mildenhall in Suffolk, where UFOs had also been sighted and recorded on radar.

The Russians certainly seemed to be taking a considerable interest in the Brawdy installations. I spoke to numerous fishermen who had seen 'Russian trawlers' prowling along the coastline near to the base, bristling with radio antennae and other detection devices, no doubt fishing more for information than for mackerel. One ex-Navy old salt had even identified a Russian submarine which surfaced in fog one early morning in the estuary just off Milford Haven.

A surveillance of Russian submarines by the Americans sounded innocent enough activity, but I was slightly sceptical of the reportage which indicated that this station at Brawdy, together with another NATO base sited on Greenland, as well as those on the American eastern seaboard, were responsible for the surveillance coverage of the North Atlantic. It seemed to me that the actual physical location of St Brides Bay, or sensors placed somewhat beyond that, would not really be sufficient to give a scan over such a wide area, as the mainland of Ireland would interrupt the view of most of the area and prevent triangulation.

The openness and quickness of the statement regarding the American role in Wales had also been in contradiction to the low-profile operations. Local residents complained to me of huge US Air Force transport planes flying into the base accompanied by double-rotored helicopters.* There certainly seemed to be a lot of activity going on internally while the external image remained almost non-existent, in contrast to the normal profile of American NATO services.

It was quite likely that submarine surveillance was one of the tasks that was being undertaken by the installation but I was convinced that this was not the end of the story. Apart from any other reason, the techniques indicated were rather out of date and did not sound like the latest technology at work; it all suggested another cover story along with the RAF presence supposedly for 'training purposes'.

Back in 1963 I had analysed two orbital paths which I suspected some form of alien space station was employing in order to survey our planet on a permanent basis. This research had been based on hundreds of UFO sightings. I suspected that there were at least two space stations and that

* A technique known to be used by the Nuclear Emergency Search Team (NEST) to recover radio-active debris.

they were in orbits which formed great circles and took the form of a sine-wave when plotted on the conventional world map. It just so happened that the particular orbit which I had worked out for the surveillance of the Soviet Union also passed directly over St Brides Bay and in brief it followed this course: St Brides Bay, Norway (near Bergen), Pechenga on the USSR border, Novaya Zemlya USSR (over the Kara Sea), across the USSR passing near Tura and Kirensk through Manchuria, North Korea and Japan via the US island of Guam, south through the Solomon Islands across the Pacific and up through South America via Mendoza and Brazil and then across the Atlantic, the Welsh coast at St Brides Bay being the first landfall again. This orbit, together with another set nearly at right angles and crossing northern Ireland, north of Birmingham UK, Calais France, Italy, Egypt, Ethiopia and Mogadiscio Somalia, down across the Indian Ocean and up through the Pacific near the French Austral Islands and through Lower California, Mexico, Arizona, Denver, Canada, and Cape Farewell Greenland, returning across the northern tip of the Republic of Ireland to its starting point and crossing the first orbit in the region of North Wales, would effectively survey most of the countries in the world with advanced technology. To do this the space stations or satellites would have to be at a good height, i.e. several hundred miles in order to obtain a sufficient horizon.

It seemed to me that the coincidence of UFO activity at St Brides Bay exactly on one of these calculated orbits and over thirteen years after I had originally calculated them, was more than just the result of good luck. Indeed the arrival of the intense UFO activity was coincidental with the coming of the American facility at St Brides Bay or vice versa. The question arose as to who was observing whom and if indeed the arrival of the one was related to the other? Were the Americans watching the UFOs or were the UFOs watching the Americans? Either way there seemed a likely connection with orbital paths of satellites and there remained the distinct possibility that the US installation was not just concerned with the Atlantic Ocean but could well be concerned with Russian or American activity in space.

The military services and NASA have more experience of and access to UFO sightings than any other body in the western world, by virtue of their continual operations in and above the atmosphere which afford them excellent observation.

In December 1977 the White House officially asked NASA to undertake a preliminary survey into how UFOs might be investigated. However, this was refused, leaving the matter in the hands of the military. The White House letter was dated 21 December 1977 and read as follows:

Honourable Frank Press
Director
Office of Science and Technology Policy
Executive of the President
Washington D.C. 20500

Dear Frank,

In response to your letter of 14 September 1977 regarding NASA's possible role in UFO matters, we are fully prepared at this time to continue responding to public inquiries along the same lines as we have in the past. If some new element of hard evidence is brought to our attention, in the future, it would be entirely appropriate for a NASA laboratory to analyse and report upon an otherwise unexplained organic or inorganic sample; we stand ready to respond to any bona-fide physical evidence from credible sources. We intend to leave the door clearly open for such a possibility.

We have given considerable thought to the question of what else the United States might and should do in the area of UFO research. There is an absence of tangible or physical evidence available for thorough laboratory analysis. And because of the absence of such evidence, we have not been able to devise a sound scientific procedure for investigating these phenomena. To proceed on a research task without a disciplinary framework and an exploratory technique in mind would be wasteful and probably unproductive. I do not feel that we could mount a research effort without a better starting point than we have been able to identify thus far. I would therefore propose that NASA take no steps to establish a research activity in this area or to convene a symposium on this subject.

I wish in no way to indicate that NASA have come to any conclusion about these phenomena as such; institutionally, we retain an open mind, a keen sense of scientific curiosity, and a willingness to analyse technical problems within our competence.

Very truly yours,
Robert A. Frosch, Administrator

A study of Unidentified Flying Objects is nowadays no longer the prerogative of 'nutcases', enthusiastic amateurs and people of eccentric leanings. It has become a subject of military interest and embarrassment. In my researches I have personally received requests for information on the subject from as far afield as the USSR Public Library of Science and Technology, the Institute of Clinical and Experimental Medicine, the Academy of Medical Sciences of the USSR, and from researchers – some civilian, some not – in Israel, the United States, Sweden, France, Italy, Brazil, Rhodesia, Australia, Holland, Ireland, Germany, Japan, South Africa, New Zealand, Canada and the United Kingdom.

The scientific, technological and economic potential of the first person or country to achieve meaningful contact with a civilization or culture more advanced than ours here on earth is inestimable.

The single events of UFO sightings, landings and activities can not be viewed individually and in isolation. They relate to wide-ranging patterns, great circles and orbital paths which completely enwrap this planet. Occasionally, in one small area, a complete gamut of activity breaks out in an intense 'flap' which leaves science incredulous and officialdom bewildered. This is the case in West Wales. It is not just a local situation, but is representative of much wider phenomena.

West Wales is important, because it is on a particular orbital path that crosses not only the United Kingdom but most of Scandinavia, the majority of the Soviet Union, and South America. The same UFO that can be sighted flying lazily over Broad Haven may the following day show up over Mendoza in Argentina. One must remember the capabilities not only of the technology with which one is supposedly dealing but also our own advances which enable us to orbit a man around the world in under two hours.

The times and the places might be greatly removed but linked they *are*. To analyse these factors various organizations are spending vast amounts of money and effort. The people who report the individual sightings may be very small and insignificant personalities, but it is a big game in which they find themselves involved.

7

The Cows Jumped Over the Moon

On 5 October 1977 Jane and I were again on the road, travelling to Wales. Our first week's stay in Pembrokeshire back in the summer had proved inadequate for coming to any conclusion over the 'Welsh Triangle'; hence, having returned from our initial investigation, we now planned to stay for six months to get to know the area and its people very well.

Our first visit was again to Ripperston Farm in order to discover if any further events had occurred since our previous discussions. Billy and Pauline Coombs had some time ago become tired of the relentless inquiries and had kindly agreed to keep any new experiences to themselves until we could talk with them again. This was indeed the case and strange things had been happening down on the farm.

I already knew from our former interviews that Billy had noted various physiological reactions in his herd of 158 Friesians during the period of most intense UFO activity. This had become evident by a marked decrease in the milk yield of the herd at that period, somewhere in the order of 15 per cent overall. Other strange behaviour in the cattle had also been noticed. The two fields where UFO landings had occurred, the first where the UFO crew had landed over the waterpipes and the second where they had apparently inserted their 'red box', the cattle now refused to enter. It was with great difficulty that Billy could bring them anywhere near the fields in question, for as soon as they approached the two respective gateways they immediately turned and stampeded in the opposite direction. There was no explicable reason for this, nothing visible that could have spooked them, but whether they were responding to some ultra-high-frequency sound or just an instinctive sense of alienation was difficult to say.

There had been numerous other incidents on the farm, many of which we shall deal with in chapter 9, on electromagnetic effects, but one of the most puzzling events had involved the same herd of 158 cows.

Billy Coombs is a particularly conscientious herdsman. He spends many nights alone with his animals, assisting the heifers through their pregnancies and tending the occasional sick animal. It was during one of these late evenings that there was a most strange occurrence. Billy had gone down to the milking complex at about ten o'clock and found that he would be needed there for several hours to watch over some heifers that were causing concern. The milking complex is a large concrete and asbestos building, not unlike an aircraft hangar though not as large, in which the cows live throughout the winter months. It is divided into several internal paddocks and adjoins the milking parlour through which twice daily the animals file strictly in order of herd seniority.

Billy had been down at the milking complex for a couple of hours and at about midnight he decided that he could leave his charges for a short while and grab a quick cup of tea up at the farmhouse. So, leaving the cows securely inside their bolted steel barriers, he walked across the well-lit concrete yard and up to the solid, cosy warmth of the farmhouse, expecting nothing unusual. He covered the distance in less than a minute, but as he walked in at the door he heard the phone ringing. Answering the call, he found that it was from a farmer friend of his who lived about a mile away. The voice on the other end of the phone sounded concerned and even slightly annoyed. Billy listened patiently as his friend told him that he had better come down to the farm and get his cows back, as they must have wandered into his fields and were now amongst his crop, happily eating. Billy told him not to be 'so dull' as he had just left the herd safely locked up in the milking complex. To get to his friend's farm they would have had to walk past him on his way up to the farmhouse, for there is no other exit from the farm. However, his friend was insistent that Billy's cows were down there in his fields a mile away over hedges, ditches and lanes, eating their way through his profit. So Billy agreed to go back and check that they were all safely inside his building, and to count them.

Somewhat amused and muttering slightly under his breath, Billy returned to the milking complex, expecting to find everything exactly as he had left it only a few minutes ago. To his amazement he looked in at a completely empty building. He couldn't believe his eyes. It was impossible for 158 cows to file out of the building within such a short

110

period of time, as they always filed in strict order. Even when walking the few yards to the milking parlour, they would have taken many minutes to cover even that short distance. But the building was completely bare!

Billy hurriedly returned to the phone, apologizing to his neighbour, but declaring his complete inability to understand what had happened. He immediately summoned assistance from his sons and departed to the other farm in order to herd his animals back to Ripperston. When he arrived he indeed found that these were his cows and to his complete amazement the other farmer further informed him that they had been down in his field for half an hour. Billy declared that this was completely impossible as he had left them for only a few minutes and had been far too busy to fall asleep. Apart from that, when he had left the milking complex at midnight for his cup of tea, all the animals had been in the building munching contentedly at their hay.

It took Billy and his sons some time to herd the animals back along the darkened lanes to Ripperston Farm and to house them safely in their covered yard. Billy couldn't understand it. None of the members of the household had heard the cattle go by and anyway it was impossible for the herd to have got past him without his noticing. Then there was the question of the time. It would have taken them at least half an hour, possibly an hour, to reach the place where they had been found and yet he had been with them supposedly at the time his friend said they had been down in his field. What could have happened?

We discussed it together over and over. There was no rational explanation. Not only had the cows mysteriously vanished from inside a concrete building secured with steel gates and steel safety bolts, but they had covered a distance of nearly a mile which would have required negotiating various lanes and opening other field gates all by themselves! Then again there was the absolutely inexplicable missing half hour. There had been no mix-up in identification of the cows: Billy knew every one by sight and, anyway,

111

they were numbered. The only explanation that seemed possible was that in some curious and unaccountable manner the cows had completely vanished from the milking complex and rematerialized over a mile away. This alone was startling enough, but there was also the fact of the complete loss of time and coordination of events.

Earlier that year, on 24 May, an event with similar characteristics had occurred in the northern desert area of Chile in South America. A seven-man unit of the Chilean Army on cavalry patrol in the desert area was camped overnight, when at ten minutes past four in the morning the man on duty suddenly saw two bright lights in the sky. He immediately woke the commanding NCO, Corporal Armando Valdes, who roused the rest of the men in order that they might observe the two brilliant objects which had now dropped towards the desert and were hovering some 500 yards from their camp. Apprehensively the Corporal ordered his men to 'stand shoulder to shoulder and do not move', while he himself edged slowly towards the lights which were now so brilliant that they illuminated a large area of the surrounding foothills.

Then suddenly, and witnessed by all six of the men looking on, their Corporal completely disappeared into thin air. The men, perplexed and uncertain what to do, stood their ground and followed their instructions. They called out to their companion, but there was no reply. However, quite without warning and only fifteen minutes later, he just reappeared near to the lights where he had vanished and as the soldiers remember: 'He came towards us and he was laughing. Then he lost consciousness and slumped to the ground. When he recovered he stood up, looked at us as if he did not know us and kept repeating, "the light, the light". Then in a strange flat voice he said, "You will never know who we are or where we came from but we will return again." After that he shook his head a couple of times and returned to normal.'

More than this, in the short fifteen-minute period

Armando Valdes had been absent, he had grown a considerable beard and his wristwatch had advanced five days.

So concerned were the Chilean authorities over the incident that they initially banned the printing of the story from their newspapers but as the story leaked out they withdrew their press censorship and allowed the men to be interviewed by Professor Pedro Araneda of Arica University. The professor stated: 'The men were apparently completely sincere in describing what they believe they saw. Whatever happened and whatever the explanation may be, it must have been an extremely unsettling experience.'

A Chilean Army spokesman said: 'We are not prepared to comment on the men's story, and so far nobody has come forward with an explanation which could account for whatever happened out there in the desert.'

Whatever did happen, it occurred in close proximity to two UFOs which either engineered or in some way triggered the event. But the unfortunate soldier is not the only person to have experienced a speeding-up of time during a UFO encounter. Indeed many witnesses have returned from contact with UFO occupants remembering experiences that took several hours and yet they had been missed for only a short while by their friends or relatives. Presumably by some mechanism that we do not understand, relativity can work both ways, causing time to shift either faster or slower; but in the case of Leia de Camargo we may never know, for she mysteriously vanished fifteen days before the Chilean desert incident. Leia, a beautiful blonde four-year-old girl, lived on the San Remo agricultural estate at Miracatu, State of São Paulo, Brazil. The estate is occupied by some thirty families, spread over a large area covered mainly in forest and abounding in small rivers. The de Camargo family are woodcutters by trade and live near the Adventist Church among other huts on a low hill.

On the morning of 9 May Mrs de Camargo and three of her daughters set out to visit a friend, Mrs de Silva, some two kilometres away and reached by a narrow rutted track.

They arrived at the friend's home at lunchtime and Leia, with her older sisters and the three de Silva girls, went outside.

At 2.15 p.m. Leia came into the house for coffee and bananas, after which the children went out again to play, watched by Leia, who sat only twenty metres from the house, happily amusing herself. She was in clear sight of Mrs de Camargo and her friend who saw her there at 2.30 p.m. It was at this time that both the mothers noticed a very peculiar 'black cloud' which approached and covered the sun. It was a very odd-looking cloud, clearly defined, broad at the base and narrowing towards the top. As the two mothers chatted together the area was shaken by two violent and terrifying explosions that sounded like tremendous claps of thunder. However, no storm followed and no lightning was seen to have caused this, but when they looked out again Leia had completely vanished. The mothers looked anxiously for the child, fearing that a storm might follow shortly. They shouted to the other children to help find her as quickly as possible, searching all over the area and calling her name loudly, but there was no sign of the little girl at all.

Fearing now for Leia's safety, the entire San Remo estate was alerted and every family joined in the search around the de Silva house. They checked every building, gully and stream, but there was no trace of the missing child. The search extended into the night, with groups searching the area with torches; at daylight they were joined by a special operations company of the São Paulo military police, who combed the entire area for three days and nights, but no sign of Leia or any of her clothing has ever been found.

The estate is an extremely small, closely knit community and any strangers in the area would certainly have been noticed by the children or the men about their work, but nobody unusual had been seen that day and there was absolutely no explanation. Foul play was not suspected and the nature of her disappearance was a complete mystery. Only one thing was certain. She had vanished at the exact

114

moment of the 'thunder claps' and afterwards the strange black cloud had not been seen in the sky. It too had completely disappeared along with Leia.

A similar black cloud had been seen in England over the primary school at Steeple Ashton, in March 1977. Mrs Ann Pritchard observed it as it glided silently across the sky. She recalls: 'It was a great big dark circle. It was enormous. It came from the direction of Westbury White Horse and disappeared into the clouds towards Semington. It happened at about 8.55 a.m., and children arriving at school dashed from the cloakroom to watch.' It was also seen by teacher Valerie Morris who said that it resembled a huge smoke ring, slightly thicker at the top and the base. She remembers: 'It was dark grey and black, and was travelling fairly fast. I don't think it could have been smoke because it kept its formation and didn't change shape at all. It was inexplicable, which does make one think of UFOs. It was just the strangeness. There was no bang with it or anything. I have never seen anything like it.'

Certainly one unfortunate gentleman who apparently came back to us in June 1950 had suffered some kind of relativity accident or journey. It occurred in Times Square, New York. A man suddenly appeared from nowhere in the middle of the heavy traffic and stood in the middle of the road intersection, gazing in amazement at the electric signs. Apparently many people saw him and described him as dressed in the manner of a gentleman of many years ago, with silk hat, cut-away coat, black and white checked trousers and buttoned shoes. Suddenly he appeared to appreciate his predicament and, unnerved by the onslaught of heavy traffic, he frantically tried to dodge the oncoming cars; but before anyone could help him, he was knocked down by a taxi and killed.

At the morgue his clothes were searched for identification and a bill from a livery stable at a Lexington Avenue was found, invoicing 'to feeding and stabling one horse and washing one carriage $3'.

The gentleman had been carrying $70 in very old-style currency notes, two gold certificates and a card bearing the name Rudolph Fentz, with an address at Fifth Avenue. None of these artefacts showed any signs of ageing and were apparently brand new, although the notes had been out of print for many years.

The police investigated and found that the Fifth Avenue address was now a store and that the present owners had no recollection of any livery stable or of a Rudolph Fentz. The name could not be traced in any directory or list of residents and no relatives called at the New York morgue to claim the body of the dead man in 1950. Finally an exhaustive search of archives found that the missing persons file of Florida in 1876 recorded a missing Rudolph Fentz. Mrs Fentz had reported that she did not like her husband smoking in the house and that she had sent him out for a walk during which he had mysteriously and inexplicably disappeared. Her description of her husband's clothing tallied exactly with that of the man killed seventy-four years later in New York.

Either a strange set of coincidences involving somebody slightly deranged and wearing fancy dress in Times Square, or a clear case of time travel? Whether the unfortunate Mr Fentz had fallen into some kind of time warp or hole in space will never be known, but certainly in his case no UFO seemed to be present, so was it just a cosmic accident?

However, some alien intelligence seems to have been responsible for an instance that occurred in a village school in East Anglia. The caretaker sighted a strange orange light in the school field one night at 10.30. The next day one of the boys found a small, plastic 'toy pistol' in the field where the UFO had been seen and took it to his teacher.

The teacher recalls: 'I popped it into my drawer until such time as someone claimed it. Near the end of the afternoon of hectic pre-Christmas activities I felt that I could not tolerate the ceaseless chatter of one Sandra and on impulse I pointed the pistol at her and said, "gottya". To my astonishment she immediately vanished. The other children, conditioned to ignore her perpetual trivialities, didn't even notice.

'At the end of the session I dismissed the class and sat down in the ill-lit room to ponder over the unprecedented situation. I was suddenly aware of the figure of a man standing by me, dressed in some kind of "boiler suit" protective clothing. I assumed he was a parent on his way home from work. He extended his hand, lying in the palm of which was another "toy pistol". Wordlessly I passed the first one over to him. He examined it briefly, clicked a small ratchet at the side, pointed it towards the corner of the room and pulled the trigger.

'To my utter amazement Sandra reappeared immediately, in full spate, breaking off only to observe that it was time to go home. And as I sat there Sandra and the stranger independently disappeared into the evening gloom.'

The 'Welsh Triangle' is no exception to strange disappearances. One incident that had been reported before Christmas 1967 is an example of the inexplicable. A flight of four Hunter aircraft out of RNAS Brawdy were practising formation flying over St Brides Bay. The weather conditions were considered good and the cloud base did not present any difficulties with visibility as the four aircraft, each containing one instructor and one student, practised their manoeuvres. Suddenly one of the aircraft touched the wing of another and the mid-air collision sent both aircraft spinning towards the ground. The senior pilot instructor observed this collision, but was relieved to see four ejector seats, two from each aircraft, shoot away from the damaged planes and four parachutes deploy perfectly as the now empty aircraft plummeted seawards. The leader dived rapidly through the cloud base, as is normal procedure, to observe where his ditching pilots would land in the waters below. He came out of his dive in good time to see two parachutes glide through the cloud down to the sea, but he waited in vain for the other two. His visibility was completely unrestricted on all sides for miles around and he was perplexed as to where the other two pilots and their parachutes could have gone. The sea was relatively calm and there was no sign of them down already; anyway there was no reason why they should have out-accelerated their two companions. But they had completely disappeared and were never found.

It seems that around the world there could be certain areas where the time-spatial cohesion is weak, and where it is possible to jump distances without the normal process of travelling from A to B. This happened to a schoolteacher in the town of Campinas, Brazil. The facts are simple but the event is fascinating. He was sitting quietly in his car alone in a football field in Pondonia. Suddenly he felt what he could only describe as a 'strange sensation' and without memory or recollection he found himself hours later over 2,000 kilometres away, minus his car. How he had covered this distance without means of transport or what had happened to him in the meantime is not known but his car was found just where he had left it when he was sitting parked in the football field. The incident had occurred shortly before the disappearance of Leia de Camargo also in the month of June 1977.

If indeed it is possible for people to fall into holes in space and time then one may speculate that one day somebody will look up to see two bewildered Navy pilots floating down from a clear blue sky on their parachutes just as they had baled out from their Hunter jets over St Brides Bay some years earlier.

Fantastic and farcical as it may sound, this actually happened in Russia, where it is reported that a woman parachutist while making a normal practice jump failed to reach the ground. A thorough search was made and no sign of her body or the parachute could be found, but astoundingly, five months later, she came floating down from the sky still on her parachute and none the worse for her incredible experience. She claims that she had been picked up in mid-air by a UFO, treated to their hospitality for a period of time and then dropped over the same place five months later.

118

I see the 'Welsh Triangle' not as a strictly geographically definable area where on one side of a line events do occur and on the other side they do not, for this would be simplistic fallacy. The fact remains that within this area more strange events occur than elsewhere, and more regularly and more spectacularly.

However, the 'triangle' is not in the horizontal plane, but the vertical; and it can be understood by assuming that the originators of it lie elsewhere, somewhere aloft at its apex in the sky. For the moment we shall content ourselves with analyzing the base of the triangle and the two points on which that base hinges, for those two points were to become very clearly defined and obvious.

8

The Gates of Uforia

The scene: again Ripperston Farm; present, the entire Coombs family; the date, early November 1977 and the occasion, a discussion of some startling events!

Pauline Coombs said: 'It's incredible, what we're going to tell you. Believe me, I know that. But all we can do is to tell you the truth. To begin with, I never minded what people might think about what was happening here – I just blurted out what I'd seen because I was so terribly frightened and bewildered. I wish I hadn't now, even though so many people have seen similar things. How could people believe what we're going to tell you? Of course they couldn't.'

The event she related had occurred on the afternoon of 30 October and had been the most startling so far. Pauline had been driving back from Talbenny accompanied by her mother, Frances Grycz, and four of the family: Katrina, aged fifteen, Kieron, and the younger twins Layanne and Joanne. She had decided to take the short cut via Broadmoor Farm and so, turning off by the disused airfield, she drove along the rutted dirt road down the valley and towards the sea and then, turning sharply left, climbed the steep hill towards Ripperston overlooking the dramatic coastal terrain. The afternoon was clear, the visibility perfect and the family in a happy mood, the children laden with sweets and goodies from the day's shopping.

Pauline recalls: 'I was driving up the back road to the farm, with all the children in the car, when we saw another enormous disc fly over us . . .'

The disc, glinting in the sun, could have been no more than 40 or 50 ft above the road as it glided silently over the fields ahead of them straight towards the mysterious Stack Rocks. The disc lost altitude and moved behind the rocks. 'Then we saw it reappear, circle the rock and – I swear this is true, we all saw it – it vanished into the rock between two doors that seemed to slide open. We couldn't believe our eyes. We saw it fly straight into those rocks. We all winced, expecting an enormous explosion, but nothing happened.' The family nodded in agreement to Pauline's statement and more details emerged as I probed the startling revelation.

Stack Rocks Island rises in three sheer and jagged pieces to a height of eighty-seven feet above sea level and is situated half a mile offshore. It is directly overlooked by Ripperston Farm and is clearly seen from the road upon which the family had been driving; this I carefully ascertained by personal inspection. The island is uninhabited and deserted and is unobserved except from the surrounding fishing villages on the bay, several miles away. At a cursory glance it is populated only by seabirds that perch precariously, huddled against the Atlantic winds, on the grey imposing rockfaces. The sea around the rocks is notorious for a heavy swell and strong currents but is peculiarly calm on the shore side, rarely giving rise to 'white horses' but presenting an extremely difficult and hazardous landing to any would-be intrepid explorer. The island is privately owned by Rose Granville, the owner of the Haven Fort Hotel, who had previously seen strange activity in the vicinity of the rocks. The Granvilles do not encourage visitors to the rocks because of the dangerous landing needed to get on to the island. The potholed and rugged coastal cliffs, dramatic in their wild beauty, are accessible only by the Pembrokeshire coastal path, maintained by the National Park Trust, which affords hikers and the general public free access to the area immediately opposite the rocks. From here the dramatic contours of the island can be clearly studied.

Pauline went on: 'Anyway, we parked the car and we all walked along the coastal path to the best vantage point for the rocks and we all saw the "door" again and this time two silvery figures walking on the edge of the rock. Then, after a bit, they retreated inside the rock.'

By this time the strange disc-like craft was no longer visible, having retreated into the bowels of the earth through the huge sliding doors in the vertical rockface. The figures had appeared after its descent and were again the typical 'astronaut' giants seen earlier in the year. They wore the same one-piece silver suits, each with a tinted dark visor on a helmet completely covering the head. They were clearly visible from the mainland and Pauline only regretted that other people were not there to witness the scene. However, her account was later corroborated, as I shall relate.

Two of the figures had emerged from inside the doors and walked down what appeared to be steps or at least step-like indentations in the dark rock to the seashore, where they appeared to be examining something. They stayed for only a few minutes and then one of the figures went up again to the doors and appeared to be working or moving about just inside the aperture. The other figure joined him after a time and the doors slid silently shut. The figures did not reappear. The family were completely stunned and startled but unsure

121

what to do, remembering their former harassing experiences with press and public.

Billy Coombs, who unfortunately had not been present at this, the high point so far, added: 'We got so tired of some of our local newspaper people making us out to be liars in the beginning and trying to trip us up with awkward questions, like we'd made it all up. We even reached a stage where we were prepared to go through truth-drug tests just to prove it! We didn't, as it turned out, but we kept everything else that happened to us a secret after that – until now, of course – for fear of being ridiculed.'

The family had then returned to the farmhouse, pondering the meaning of it all and the incredibility of their position. As they entered the farmhouse the telephone had started to ring. The call was from Rose Granville, the owner of the island.

Pauline remembers: 'She said, "You'll never guess what I've just seen", and proceeded to describe how she and her family also had witnessed the strange event.'

Jane and I visited Rose and her family later and she confirmed everything in detail. They had been sitting in the lounge of their hotel which, perched as it is on the high clifftop, commands an impressive panoramic view of the bay and the ocean, when their attention had been drawn seawards by a flash, possibly the sun glinting off the polished surface of the 'saucer' seen by Pauline and her family. The flash had come from the direction of their islands and, wondering what it could have been, Rose had fetched her powerful binoculars and studied the small knoll on the horizon. She was amazed to see the figures emerge and come down to the water's edge, just as Pauline had described. She passed the binoculars to her daughter Francine and husband Hayden. They confirmed the sighting and watched with wonder as the figures later retreated deep underground. The only person Rose could think of phoning was Pauline, as she already knew of her experiences. She at least would believe she was telling the truth. They were delighted to find that they could confirm each other's account.

It is fortunate indeed that Rose and her family had been in the lounge at that time, for the island is not easy to see from the village of Little Haven which nestles in a small inlet. However, from the Haven Fort Hotel the visibility across the bay is unobstructed and the two sightings confirmed that the entrance to the underground installation, for that is what it appeared to be, was situated on the shoreward side of the largest of the three sections of Stack Rocks Island, facing roughly southeast and at some considerable height above the level of the ocean.

There was no question of the genuineness of the witnesses. The Granville family had no incentive to seek any notoriety for their offshore islands and Pauline's mother, Mrs Grycz, who confirmed the report as I ascertained on a later visit, was a very down-to-earth middle-aged Englishwoman (deriving her surname from her Polish husband). Both were concerned only with the welfare of their children and the day-to-day running of their home in Milford Haven.

Pauline and Billy told me of other occasions when they had seen the disc near to the rocks. Twice they had watched the strange craft actually dive underwater close to the rocks and not reappear, and it seemed that the islands themselves might be concealing some larger facility underground and under the sea. Local scuba divers I interviewed confirmed that the rocks and the coastline are indented with submerged sea caves and crevices, many of which are unexplored, and that the area close to the rocks has an incredibly strong current which does not encourage investigation by the local men. However, visibility is crystal clear in the unpolluted Atlantic tidal stream.

One diver recalled hearing a strange, indefinable underwater humming somewhere near the area.

What more evidence did we need, the islands held a mystery and a secret beyond one's imagination!

Pauline expressed my thoughts for me. 'Stack Rocks. We

now reckon that's where they are coming from. Whatever their interest – whether it is to study human life here, in a desolate undisturbed spot, or whether it is to study scientific developments and military installations at the US Underwater Radar Research Station up the coast, or at the Brawdy Air Base – those rocks would be the ideal place to be based. And there's definitely something happening there.'

Billy taxied me down through the thick mud of winter across the fields to the coastal path. It was cold, the full bite of winter roaring in from the Atlantic beyond. We stood together on the coastal path, the rain lashing our faces, the seabirds mocking at us above our heads, the island beyond. Stack Rocks before us: grey, unyielding and shrouded in mystery. I toyed with the idea of hiring a boat. The sea persuaded me differently. There must have been a nine-foot swell running. The wind was touching force 8. What an ideal spot, I thought to myself. A fortress: remote, not overlooked, an undisturbed retreat.

I looked beyond, across the bay. Seven miles distant, unobstructed over open water, a fleeting glint of weak sunlight streaked through dark clouds, catching the low white buildings of the American Underwater Research Base and RAF Brawdy. It was indeed an ideal spot. No aircraft were flying that day, the weather was too poor. There was nothing more to be done for the moment, so we climbed back into the diesel tractor and bumped and squelched our way through the red mud back to the farmhouse. From the kitchen window the rock was still visible. We looked at it again. Would it yield its secret? I thought not. It seemed too deeply buried, too well planned, well chosen, impregnable. Guarded by wind and tide, protected by the violence of nature herself as expressed in the ceaseless onslaught of the Atlantic weather.

Back in the sitting-room a huge log fire warmed us, reassuring and familiar. Clinton, Billy and Pauline's elder son, joined us and confirmed that he also had seen strange openings in the rock. Kieron too had seen them on other

124

occasions, and also the twins. Whatever was there had been present for several months, possibly longer.

The whole scene took on an air of unreality. I stared into the flames and tried to absorb the atmosphere. Here we were, sitting in a Welsh farmhouse built of solid slate and constructed some centuries ago, talking with amiable, hospitable country people who had no interest at all in the far-out recesses of space, and even less in strange military experiments and political intrigues. And yet one mile distant from where we were sitting had been discovered possibly the first UFO base on earth: the first installation, whether small or large, permanent or temporary, where without question some technology beyond that of mankind's had seemed to establish itself on the surface of this planet.

Only a little farther across the bay the enigmatic research installations posed deeper and equally ponderous mysteries. I felt we were at the 'Gates of Uforia'. Now we had found the two base points of the 'Welsh Triangle', upon which all events hinged; but greater than these, where in the stars was the apex?

9

Microwave Days, Ultraviolet Nights and Radio Snow

On 7 February 1977 the editor of the *Daily Mirror* had been kind enough to publish a letter from me asking people who had ever seen an Unidentified Flying Object to write to me and tell me about their experiences. I was overwhelmed with more than 2,000 replies. The letter I had written to the *Daily Mirror* had been in response to a series of articles by Michael Hellicar entitled 'Is Someone Up There Watching Us?'

The article which had appeared on 31 January carried a

125

fascinating account by a Mr and Mrs S who wished to remain anonymous as they feared that their names being associated with a UFO sighting could possibly reflect on their public life. However, the article assured us that they were extremely respectable citizens of unquestionable integrity.

The article stated that on the night of Wednesday, 5 January 1977 Mr and Mrs S had been taking their spaniel, Flop, for an evening stroll. The air was clear and the moon was full, giving excellent visibility. Their suspicions had first been aroused by the unnatural growls of the spaniel. Turning to see what was worrying him, they had observed hovering over a neighbouring field a huge, grey saucer-shaped object.

Mr S stated: 'The saucer was about 100 yards away at a height of 80 ft. We could see it clearly and there is no way it could have been a balloon, a low cloud, stray washing or even a hoax. Its size was overwhelming, the height of a double-decker bus. And I estimated its diameter as 50 ft. There was no noise, in fact it seemed all the more eerie and menacing by just hovering in total silence. There were no lights, windows or doors and no markings. The underneath was partly in shadow, but I am certain there were no wheels or legs.

'We just stood there, holding each other in sheer terror. Neither of us spoke or moved and we quite forgot we were so cold. After about twenty minutes the saucer suddenly took off. There was no noise, no jet stream. It seemed to lift itself into the sky – incredibly fast, faster than anything I have ever seen – and in a fraction of a second it had gone.'

Upon returning home the worried couple found that their television set had been registering inexplicable interference. Their twenty-one-year-old son had been watching for half an hour previously and the screening had been upset by waves of electrical interference for which he could find no cause and which ceased as soon as the UFO had departed. During the sighting Flop the spaniel had made off in complete panic

126

and was only found two days later in a village four miles away, totally exhausted and hungry.

Mr S further reported: 'The following night we were watching TV when the picture broke up into zigzag lines. I ran to the window, pulled aside the blinds – and there was the saucer again. I just had time to see that it was in the same place and at the same height as the night before. A split second later it flew upwards and vanished.'

On two occasions the UFO had returned to an identical location in the field adjoining Mr and Mrs S's property. On both occasions it had produced noticeable interference on the television set which had caused the picture to break up into a disconnected series of lines, the same as in the encounter when Pauline Coombs's 'giant' had affected the family's television set in Wales. Mr S is a senior civil servant and had no motive for concocting such a story. Furthermore he lives in close proximity to Lakenheath and Mildenhall US Air Force Base in Suffolk. Again the common denominators were present: the UFO had been seen outside but in a position to observe an important NATO base apparently unrecorded on RAF radar and unobserved by the air defence network. On both occasions the television set had registered the UFO's presence; this same disruption of the incoming signal could also be caused by some magnetic field which made the object invisible to the radar network.

The connection between UFOs and electromagnetic interference is very strong and in our discussions with our key witnesses in the 'Welsh Triangle' the effects became even more dramatic.

During our interview with Terry and Sandra Marston, whose son Mark had encountered one of the 'giants' near the village of Herbrandston, Terry had told us of power overloads occurring in the village. Apparently throughout the period of UFO activity the overload trip switch in the house had often cut out quite inexplicably and without any electrical apparatus appearing to be at fault. Despite a complete checking of the circuitry, the fault had recurred frequently and was not uncommon to other residents in the remote village. Fuses also blew and light bulbs had a notoriously short life, sometimes in an evening several failing simultaneously.

Interference of a more intense order had also been experienced by the Coombs family at their remote coastal farmhouse. At first they had not associated a succession of electrical failures with UFOs but as time went on the coincidence became unquestionable. Pauline and Billy told me that their household economy was a thrifty one. They did not have central heating but relied on log fires in the winter and oil stoves to heat individual rooms. Their electrical consumption amounted to one electric cooker, a refrigerator, a black and white television set, one convector fire sparingly used, and the electric immersion heater which Pauline had on only twice a week. But despite all their care they were suffering a continuous and ridiculously heavy power drain. Fortunately for their budget Pauline uses a 50p slot meter, but even so, it was not uncommon for her to spend over £60 on electricity in a month. As consumers will know, even with electric central heating it is very unlikely that a small household bill would come to a figure of over £180 per quarter – which is a meagre estimate of what the Coombs household was spending. So alarmed had they become by their disastrous electricity bills that they had on occasions requested the utility to check the entire circuitry. This had proved absolutely blameless. No 'shorts' or faults could be found.

When they had been especially worried by the cost of their electricity they had made a point of switching off every single apparatus in the house as a test and checking against the electricity meter. The dial continued to rotate at high speed and yet the meter had been changed for a new unit and apparently was functioning perfectly normally.

Not only had they noticed an incredible number of power overloads, blackouts and voltage variations, but the problem had also caused numerous failures. Electric light bulbs popped and burnt out even when bought only the previous day. All kinds of electrical equipment continued to give trouble, including record players and radio sets. The record of television faults was alarming: in one year eight sets had exploded. They had used receivers both new and secondhand from various manufacturers, but after a few weeks or months all of them had failed: two of them the very next day after they had been installed. The television engineer was such a regular caller that it had become almost a joke. On one occasion a brand new Grundig black and white television receiver had been installed, equipped with an electronic tuning system; shortly afterwards it failed completely and refused to work. The set had been returned to the supplier's service depot where, after several months of working on the set, the engineers reported that they had replaced 280 individual components but the set still refused to work. Other sets had just failed and left nothing but charred interiors or burnt-out transformers and circuitry, while others literally exploded. All of these failures had occurred at times when the UFO activity had been most intense. Even Pauline's electric cooker had given trouble and seemed to suffer from power overload, with the switches occasionally smoking and the rings glowing so red and hot that she had to turn it off for fear of a serious accident.

Though the Coombs seemed to be receiving energy from somewhere, the irony of it was that its effects were most unwelcome. Not only did it cause electrical apparatus to burn out or overload, it also caused the electric meter to function at high speed when in fact no electricity was being consumed in the house. According to the TV engineer, the only explanation he could find was that the TV sets were being blown out by some intense, high-frequency electromagnetic radiation that was being picked up by the aerial and amplified by the set and was completely destroying the circuitry.

Fortunately, throughout all these alarming domestic occurrences, nobody had been hurt or suffered any ill effects.

The electrical troubles were not confined to the circuitry in the house. The milking complex has an entirely separate heavy-duty supply, separate meters and switch gear. The troubles there duplicated those of the house and also caused the circuit breakers to drop out inexplicably, fuses to blow and equipment to overload. Fortunately the electricity bill for the farm complex was paid by the holding company and not by the Coombs personally, otherwise they would have been financially hit by the high readings on the electric meters.

On the transportation side an equally alarming story emerged. None of the diesel tractors had been affected but Billy Coombs had scrapped five cars in one year: all of them had unaccountably failed due to electrical trouble, and despite complete checking out by specialists no faults could ever be specifically identified or rectified. They just refused to work. It seemed that all of the electrical insulation throughout the various components had broken down. Electric high-tension coils refused to function, distributors burnt out, light bulbs blew, radios packed up. Everything involving the use of electricity in the car eventually failed. Likewise the car that Pauline had been driving the night she was chased by the 'flying football' had eventually been sold to the scrapyard, its accumulated faults making it impractical for it to be repaired. One Ford Zodiac which Billy had been driving down the farm track to the farmhouse actually caught fire, apparently due to the overloading of electrical wiring which had set fire to the petrol. The car was a complete loss, just a burnt-out hulk after the accident.

Billy told me of one 'trick' that he had worked with a continental television receiver during an amazing period of power fluctuation which had lasted continuously for over three weeks. On several evenings in the week, at about 7.00, the electric power would start to fade. Electric bulbs would diminish to a yellow glimmer, the cooker hardly worked and the television picture was reduced and faded away to a meaningless blur. Billy had found that by going to the rear of the TV set and changing over the voltage selector from 240V to 110V the television was restored to a normal picture. This they could watch in the dim glow of their lights until about 10 o'clock. The power would then pick up again. Quickly Billy would leap to the back of the TV set and restore the voltage selector to the 240V position, to prevent the set overloading. But the amazing thing was that apparently the power was not content just to restore itself to the full capacity! It would start to go beyond 240V, for electric light bulbs would pop and the television cathode tube would begin to crackle with HT discharge. So eventually they would have to turn the set off completely, fearing another failure as had happened many times before. However, when questioned, the local electricity authority knew nothing of these gigantic fluctuations. Whatever was affecting the Coombs farm must have occurred only in the half mile of electric poles that supplied those buildings and nowhere else, for no other consumer had reported a similar fault. Again the supply and equipment were checked out but no cause was found.

The telephone was no exception in this period of electrical chaos. On occasions it would ring either once, or continuously. No caller was ever at the end of the line and it also failed with monotonous regularity. Even if it was possible to get through on the Coombs number the line often carried a very high level of interference, static and general distortion. Sometimes one could hardly hear the voice at the other end. Visits by the GPO engineer had been so regular that the family were now virtually on first names with the telephone communications staff.

It seems that whatever was happening, Ripperston Farm was subject to interference from intense electromagnetic fields. Whether this originated underground or from some aerial craft was not clear, but its effects were manifest. The television engineers had indicated that the frequency must have been extremely high to have affected the UHF TV receiver in such a way and it is even possible that this same

131

kind of field may have been affecting the cows physiologically with regard to their low milk yields and their other erratic behaviour out in the fields.

In the United States the Smithsonian Institute has set up a special committee to investigate instances where it is thought that possibly manmade radiation is affecting animals. The danger is apparently that power stations, radios, TV transmitters, and even microwave ovens could be producing electromagnetic radiation which affects animals. Dr Susan Korbel, who has been studying the effects on animals of longterm exposure to electromagnetic radiation, specifically in rats, says that there is evidence that it can break down body chemicals and affect the brain.

Possible examples are attacks by birds on people in America and Poland, an invasion of at least 20 million squirrels in the South West States of America and a suicide attack by rats on a small town in Illinois; while in Nova Scotia the inhabitants of tiny Prince Edward Island spent a week under attack from 5 million crows. Even shotguns could not scare them off.

In the Soviet Union a report from the Soviet Academy of Sciences has lent weight to Dr Krobel's theory of electromagnetic radiation affecting brain pattern characteristics. The Academy suggests that changes may be taking place in the world's biological system. A spokesman has stated: 'We are witnessing rare and unusual animal behaviour, strange migrations and sudden population explosions in insects and animals.'

Although the events might seemingly be unconnected it is possible that electromagnetic radiation can affect behaviour, possibly even genetics. Work carried out in Canada and the Soviet Union has also shown that strong electromagnetic fields can affect human behaviour, causing nausea, vomiting, disorientation and general mental unbalance. Exactly what is the biological function by which this happens is a subject of research; however, its effects have been noted under laboratory conditions for a number of years. It is not really known as yet whether it is the frequency, intensity or wave pattern of the field which produces the results. It could be purely a chemical breakdown of the body's delicate hormone functions. Even cancer research has looked at radiation as a likely cause of many of our modern ills.

Fortunately in the St Brides Bay area of West Wales, none of the key witnesses that I have interviewed so far have shown any abnormal reactions or health hazards; although the cows are obviously aware of some invisible, intangible danger.

Pauline also told me of their dog Blackie. Up until the time of the UFO encounters he was a perfectly normal black Labrador but afterwards he became cautious and neurotic, sometimes snarling at things that were not there and refusing to go out at night, when before he had often enjoyed a midnight stroll. Dogs seem to be particularly sensitive to whatever radiations are present, as in the case of Stephen Taylor's Pomeranian which had behaved oddly on Stephen's return from his close encounter; and also Louise Bassett's two dogs which had acted in complete panic and bewilderment when she returned home from witnessing the close approach of a UFO at Ferryside. She too had experienced the inexplicable television problems, along with other viewers, during the presence of the blue aerial lights.

Ultrasonic sound could also be affecting the animals' behaviour during these encounters at Ripperston Farm and elsewhere.

An alarming example had been reported to me in early 1977 from the West Country. A house was being renovated and extended, and had one section of its attic wall missing, covered only by a huge tarpaulin. The owner of the house, a Mr Bennet, was concerned because he believed the house to be haunted, for while it was empty strange things had been going on there. The house had been unoccupied for six months while the renovation work continued and Mr Bennet was living in a nearby property. On a number of occasions people had informed him that they had seen lights and heard noises coming from the house but after a thorough search of the building he found no trace of anyone; all the doors and windows had been securely fastened and showed no signs of having been forced.

However, a few days later, while looking round his garden last thing at night, he himself heard the noise: a sort of bumping sound, as of something soft and heavy being dragged downstairs. He immediately went to the empty property, let himself in and stood listening for a few minutes before going on. The noise reached him from above, so, moving carefully in the dark, as the electricity had been switched off at the start of the building work, he made his way upstairs.

As he crept up the stairway the noise became clearer, a low humming with a slight throb breaking the tone at intervals of about five seconds. When he reached the landing he was unable to determine from which direction the noise was coming, as it seemed to be all around him.

Then suddenly the noise ceased and he was left with a ringing in his ears which continued for a few minutes. Eventually, as he decided on his next move, a scraping sound reached him from the attic above. He hurried to a room where he knew a stepladder was kept and succeeded in erecting it under the loft door. Apprehensively he debated to himself whether or not to fetch help first in case he was attacked, but the humming started up again, reaching a much higher pitch than before and setting his teeth on edge.

He decided to investigate on his own, as whatever it was had now set up a strong vibration in the building. As soon as he lifted the trapdoor the noise intensified tremendously and a peculiar smell reached his nostrils like that of burning rubber, but more sickening. Then, as he looked about him, still standing on the steps, he made out a faint silvery shape at the far end of the attic near the hole in the wall. Unable to recognize what it was, he climbed up into the attic, but as he did so, a luminous glow came from the shape. Without warning a beam of light hit him and he was unable to see anything more. He remembers falling down amongst the rafters and lying there in complete panic as all he could see was flashing lights before his eyes. He found he was unable to rise from his face-down position, some unknown force holding him there.

After a while he calmed down and was able to get into a sitting position, though when he held his wristwatch up to his face he was alarmed to find he could not see its luminous dial. He thinks he must have remained there for about five minutes before he realized that the noise had ceased and all was now quiet again. He sat still, temporarily blinded by the light and confused, not able to make out his surroundings.

He hastily scrambled out of the attic and rushed outside, still a little unsteady on his feet. He looked at the house. The heavy tarpaulin covering the wall had disappeared, presumably blown away by the wind.

Although alarmed, Mr Bennet did not inform anyone about what had happened to him, as he wasn't sure in his own mind of what he had witnessed and he did not wish to give the house a bad name. It wasn't until some six weeks later that he was informed by neighbours that on the night when he had been in the attic there was a UFO near to the empty house.

Mr Bennet's ghost had been no ghost at all, but whatever it was it had caused a huge magnetic disturbance which had ruined his wristwatch and affected other metal in the property. Later he found the missing tarpaulin with its ropes completely snapped off and lying 600 yards upwind of the property. The most baffling thing is that when tested with a compass needle it was found that even the tarpaulin had become magnetized and affected the bearing of the compass, in some way unknown.

What possible interest the UFO could have had in the attic of the empty property and why the silver-suited figure was snooping around in the dead of night has never been explained. The significant thing about the incident is that the disorientation to the witness was caused by sound. It had completely filled his ears and mind and almost prevented him from thinking because of its incessant and hypnotic throb.

Was this just another side effect of the propulsion system associated with UFOs or was it in some way used to disorientate the witness and delay him while the 'ufonaut' made a hasty retreat? These are questions to which we may never have answers, but there have been similar experiences in other parts of the world where light and sound have very successfully unnerved both military and civilian personnel when in close proximity to a hovering UFO.

Another strange and frightening phenomenon alarmed coastguard Tony Dalton at Fishguard in the Pembrokeshire Coast National Park. It occurred on 14 November 1977 at Garn Fawr, near Strumble Head.

Coastguard Dalton described 'a very large, brilliant, yellow-green transparent ball with a fuzzy outline, which descended from the base of a towering cloud over Garn Fawr mountain and appeared to float down a hillside. It emitted intense light for about three seconds and there was static on the radio.'

The coastguard stated that the object slowly rotated around a horizontal axis and seemed to bounce off projections on the ground. Cattle and seabirds in the vicinity became disturbed and it was this that first aroused his attention. He first of all thought it might be a UFO but a later explanation wrote it off as 'ball lightning'.

A spokesman for the Meteorological Office described the sighting as 'a rare case among rare cases'. Apparently ball lightning has never been seen before larger than about 6 inches in diameter but Tony Dalton's description of his object placed it as spherical and as 'big as a bus'.

Strange 'ball lightning' indeed.

High-voltage static discharge has also long been associated with UFOs. One classic case occurred in 1966 at Hamilton, Ontario. A thirteen-year-old boy, Charles Cozens, had ob-

136

served at 9.15 p.m. two objects descend which he described as '8 ft long, 4 ft wide and 3 ft high with red, blue and green lights set into the rim and flickering like a computer. The objects lit up the grass around and were making a buzzing sound.'

Charles saw the objects descend low enough for him to go up and touch them. He found them to be hard and smooth and the metal to be about body temperature. One of the objects had an antenna which he described as 'thicker at the base and narrowed to the size of a nickel at the top'. He touched it and received 'a flash of electricity'.

He then ran home, where his parents summoned the local police who verified that the boy had a three-inch yellowish burn on his hand. The police stated that the boy 'was emphatic and could not be shaken'.

Fortunately Charles Cozens suffered only a minor injury from his foolish approach to the craft. It is regrettable that this has not always been the case and in a number of isolated incidents people, mostly military personnel, have been injured when attempting to get too close to a UFO's 'force field'. Some witnesses have described feeling as if they were 'on fire'. The radiation does not seem to be of the conventional type but is present while the UFO is close and decays shortly after, apparently being caused by some HT field, ionization or magnetic effect.

These characteristics are consistent with a craft deploying some kind of field, possibly by the use of superconductors. Unfortunate witnesses approaching these craft when they have taken off and the field has increased have been hit by waves of heat and charged air. The function of the ionization would have three effects: it would tend to allow the vehicle to travel in a near vacuum if the air molecules touching the object were broken down into their component parts; it would make the vehicle very difficult to locate on radar; and it would disrupt radio and TV transmissions within its vicinity. It is often the case that craft are clearly seen by witnesses, sometimes qualified military observers, but do not show up on radar. A more intriguing characteristic is that they can at times appear on radar as perfectly solid objects undertaking normal ballistic manoeuvres, while intercepting jets or ground observers see nothing at all, the vehicle itself being invisible. Even this does not require us to stretch our imagination too far, for even in schoolboy physics one learns that light bends. Hence with an appropriate intensity of field the craft may well be modulating the photons in its vicinity so that in fact it is nearly invisible, the observer seeing a bent and distorted image of what is beyond the object, rather like an induced mirage.

One possible instance of this occurred in the 'Welsh Triangle' in the winter of 1966. Paul Weatherall, a Pembroke Dock schoolboy, was taking pictures across Neyland. They were perfectly normal panoramic shots and at no time did he witness anything unusual, but on return of his developed black and white film he was amazed to find that he had captured in the top centre of a picture a clearly defined saucer-shaped UFO surrounded by a lighter area of haze. It is very unlikely that Paul would have missed the object if it had been visible to his human eye responding to normal visible light, but it is known that black and white negative film has a high sensitivity towards the ultraviolet end of the spectrum and it is possible that he had captured an object which was visible only in this extended frequency of vision available to the camera but not to his eyes.

The object he photographed shows a central dome encircled by a flange three times wider and the whole craft is surrounded by a white hazy field trailing back in the direction from which it had presumably travelled.

The UFOs' preference for ultraviolet light was revealed in another and startling example in the 'Triangle'.

At the now UFO-haunted Ripperston Farm, Pauline Coombs was again the witness to a strange event. It occurred one night during our researches in the area although unfortunately we were not contacted immediately due to our being without a telephone link at the time. During February 1978, on two occasions Pauline Coombs had been witness late at night to another visitation from the 'giants'. On both occasions she had sighted in the dim exterior lights of the farmyard one of the 'astronauts' walking up from the coast on the track which goes past their isolated home. She watched with amazement, now resigned to the idea that no one was going to believe her or render assistance, although still hopeful that no harm would come to either her or her family as she saw the big figure in the identical dress as before, move steadily past her front garden towards the deserted aerodrome at South Hill.

She described the spaceman as having been 'surrounded by a kind of moonlight glow' and for once she thought that maybe she could see behind the darkened visor. She spoke of long, flowing fair-coloured hair coming down to about shoulder length, although specific details were still indefinable. The next day I learnt of the incident when making a routine call and hurried to extract the full story before the details slipped from her mind. When I arrived I was immediately struck by her appearance and I inquired if she had been using a sunlamp. For in the middle of winter she was showing the definite signs of a pronounced suntan. She complained to me of an irritation in her eyes and indeed it was clear that there was some swelling around them. The 'sunburn' followed the lines of her clothing and it had turned her skin overnight quite pink, with more on the side which was turned towards the 'astronaut' than the other. She became so worried by the eye irritation that she consulted her doctor. He prescribed a harmless eyewash, being somewhat at a loss to understand how she had incurred the ailment. She also complained to me of a slight rash on her arms which had been exposed at the time but this did not seem to be giving any trouble. Both rash and sunburn disappeared without complication over a few days and did not return until the second sighting of the same figure several weeks later.

During this period we were in close contact with the Coombs family and another corroborated UFO sighting took place. They had returned from having spent a pleasant evening with us over coffee discussing the strange events and had retired to bed at about 1 a.m. when the entire farmyard was lit up by a brilliant white light apparently passing overhead. No aircraft noise was heard and although they rushed to the window they were not quick enough to see the source of the strange illumination.

Quite without prompting and independently of the Coombs's sighting Rose Granville informed me the following day that she also had been 'buzzed' again at the hotel by a UFO. It had circled, illuminating the area again in eerie silence and at very much the same time as the Coombs family had reported their incident.

During the same period as these sightings occurred there was another series of events which I had not initially associated with the UFOs, but now was inclined to think there was in fact a very real connection. This was the winter of the 'whiteout'. We had all awoke one morning to find that the entire region of South Wales bordering the Pembrokeshire coast, parts of the Bristol Channel and much of the West Country had been snowed out in a tremendous blizzard. Rather than the snows clearing in the next few days a further drop in temperature occurred and the situation became totally impossible. We took pictures of 12-ft-high snow drifts down the lane leading to our cottage and motorists were marooned for days in makeshift encampments in villages on the M4 leading into West Wales. The weather conditions, which were described as the worst known for forty years, brought all traffic and transportation to a standstill, caused electrical failures and several deaths to people who were trapped in cars, suffocating as they were snowed in.

Although superficially a natural event, information came to light which caused us to question this. Earlier in the winter I had noted that Ripperston Farm and its immediate

140

area was unnaturally warm. I'm pretty sure it wasn't my imagination for if anything it should have been a lot colder than elsewhere, receiving the continuous blast of the Atlantic wind. Neither could it be explained just by the warming effect of the Gulf Stream. The area around the farm had a strange stillness and calm. Again by way of contrast, to walk only a short distance, a mile or two, towards Little Haven took one into the full blast of the coastal winds. On one occasion I drove from the Haven Fort Hotel, where the wind must have been up in the force 10 region, to find that at Ripperston Farm there was only a gentle breeze. I could make no sense of this at all; something felt wrong or arranged, even artificial. I got to thinking that maybe along with all the electromagnetic effects the air temperature could be affected by some kind of force field in that area. It might sound a crazy thought but I got the definite impression that some warming effect was causing the air there to be way above the temperature elsewhere and much more tranquil. This effect also seemed to extend to the stretch of water between the mainland and Stack Rocks, and to write it off as just the sheltering effect of the coastal cliffs seemed too simple and inadequate an explanation. Could the technology of the ufonauts under Stack Rocks control not only magnetism but also the local weather? The result was that the area was noticeably more amenable than one would expect. The snow never settled on Stack Rocks throughout the whole of the winter. An encouraging thought, that one day we might learn to control our environment and create a more pleasing and stable one than we have at the present time.

But the Coombs family had another revelation. After their initial publicity in early 1977 they had received a number of letters from interested parties. These varied from UFO societies in different parts of the world to interested individuals seeking information, and the occasional nutcase. But one letter had intrigued them. It had been sent to them by a member of the armed services and came in the form of a computer readout. The letter which constituted a message on a number of different items specifically predicted in spring 1977 that the winter of late 1977 and early 1978 would be exceptionally severe, created artificially so by Russian interference with the weather pattern. The motives of the person revealing this information seemed rather unclear and there was a vague political reference which may well have given him leanings either to the left or to the right; but at the time the letter had been put with all the other freaks.

However, later events seemed to give it more significance. The letter had been passed on to other interested parties who had apparently taken it up with the Ministry of Defence. The Ministry of Defence stated that there was absolutely nothing in it, but so emphatically that I was a little suspicious: usually a very strong reaction is almost as good as saying there is something in it. Moreover the parties to whom the letter had been given had not returned it, their explanation being that the MOD would not return it to them. The disappearance of the original document placed even more significance on its possible meaning. A copy had been returned to the Coombs which allegedly was the original but it was not, and an examination of it revealed it to be gibberish. The Coombs were certain that this was not the letter that they themselves had in fact received but was a poor and amateurish replacement supposedly to fob them off, in an attempt to convince them even more of the insignificance of the letter containing the original prediction. More specifically the original communication had stated that the Russians would produce this incredible weather by the propagation of intense radio waves. During the same period America, particularly the eastern States, was experiencing freak weather which cost millions of dollars in loss of earnings, damage and even lives.

As I could see no particular advantage in the USA's creating the extreme cold-weather conditions, I could only speculate that if indeed the story had any truth in it, it was the Russians who were creating the weather problems and the Americans might be engaged in some vain attempt to block the signal.

More information came from public denouncements in Canada of the Russian action. Scientists claimed that the Russians were sending an intense and narrow radio beam across the Pacific Ocean towards Canada. The item was featured in the *Tonight* programme on TV as well as in other news programmes. Canadian scientists claimed that the beam was so intense that it could cause physical reactions in human beings. Others claimed that the Russians had caused a build-up of frontal weather conditions which on one occasion had created storms all along the California seaboard. The story of course was hotly denied by the United States, even though they were not being blamed for it; but I often find that state secrets are mostly kept from the population itself rather than from the 'other side' – ironically for some reason more to do with 'public relations' than with national security.

More pieces of the jigsaw fitted together. Were they significant or not?

It had been reported that a trawler had dragged up a cable in St Brides Bay which was connected to the 'Oceanographic Research Station' operated by the United States Navy. The story at the time was that the cable was connected to a hydrophone, somewhere out in the Atlantic, for listening to submarines, but later reports indicated that the entire floor of St Brides Bay was crisscrossed with cables connected to the mysterious US establishment. I discussed the problem with physicists and engineers and came to the conclusion that this sounded to be something far more than a series of cables going out to a few hydrophones.

Other pieces of public information emerged which were intriguing and possibly highly significant when viewed in this new light. On the air traffic control map of southern England a specific area of St Brides Bay on the Stack Rocks side had been designated EGD111 and marked 'Danger. Restricted or Warning Area'. The classification which effectively kept out civilian aviation and reserved the area for the use of the military included the whole of the coastal region opposite Stack Rocks Island, Ripperston Farm, the village of Herbrandston, the old airfield at Talbenny, South Hill and Broad Haven primary school where the earlier reports had come from. In fact, if one examined EGD111, one found that 75 per cent of all the 'Welsh Triangle' sightings, and certainly the most spectacular occurrences, had been within its boundaries. Surely this could not just be coincidence? We had already established by the nature of the UFO observations that they were not conventional aircraft or misidentifications. Therefore we had a situation where the military had designated the exact area of intense UFO activity as being 'Restricted'. Another curiosity was that the EGD111 did not actually extend as far as RAF Brawdy's airfield but lay more to the southwest. Hence it could not be written off as just an air traffic control zone to keep private aircraft away from high-speed jets operating from that field.

Another fascinating fact emerged from a study of the air traffic control map. Ripperston Farm and Stack Rocks were almost exactly on a line down range from the main Brawdy runway, seven miles distant across the bay. If the 'ufonauts' had indeed established a base under Stack Rocks, then they had chosen an ideal site from which to monitor every single activity, arrival and departure, from the mysterious base.

Other information became apparent from readily available information. A simple measurement of the runways on the Ordnance Survey map and the air traffic control map raised a further query as to why the runways had needed to be lengthened ostensibly to take the RAF jets. Prior to its RAF takeover Brawdy had been a fully operational naval station accommodating high-speed naval aircraft. With the advent of modern fighters and retrothrust, there seemed no logical reason at all for lengthening the runway. For if every fighter aircraft in NATO required a runway of two miles,

144

the strategic potential would be vastly diminished and the number of operating stations reduced to a mere nothing. What had needed to be flown in, in the largest air transporters that could not possibly have been brought in any other way? Furthermore it was at an expense to the British taxpayer many times greater than that of building a section of motorway.

A detailed re-examination of the UFO sightings reported at close range to the NATO installations also produced other facts. As opposed to UFOs seen generally which are observed normally to carry a large number of lights or are described as luminous, all of those seen near to Brawdy on the ground or in the air as well as those near to Lakenheath and Mildenhall had been dark, unlit objects. The craft had not carried the regular red lights. They had been just dark, unmarked shells hovering silently near the secret NATO installations. Together with their trick of blacking out radar they seemed unwilling to attract attention, being content to 'sit' there and survey quietly undetected. Why were these installations being scrutinized?

Equally we do not have to single out the Americans. Large numbers of installations in the USSR have received similar treatment. In one leak of information that came out of Russia it was stated that a Russian Army missile silo commander had panicked when a formation of UFOs circled his base in Siberia. The base, which housed intercontinental ballistic missiles, had a protective cover of ground-to-air strike missiles and a battery of these had been released almost spontaneously without clearance from Moscow. They exploded and fell harmlessly back to earth before reaching the altitude of the circling saucers.

As long ago as the summer of 1944, during the Second World War, the UFOs had demonstrated an ability to shield themselves from conventional attack. During the battle for Loreto, Castelfodardo and Osimo both German and Allied troops had sighted at 10.30 a.m. an egg-shaped, metallic, glistening object which appeared in the cloudless sky and remained motionless over the opposing lines despite a strong wind. Both sides had assumed that it was a secret weapon of the other and anti-aircraft artillery had opened up with everything they had got. However, the barrage of fire proved completely ineffectual, with the shells bursting well below the object. It did not even stir until it eventually tilted at 50° and suddenly moved upwards, disappearing into the blue Italian skies. Along with the fabled 'foo-fighters', it was only after the Second World War that Allied Intelligence realized that these sightings did not refer to German secret weapons and that the Axis powers had been equally baffled by the strange appearances.

I myself had known one Squadron Leader of a bomber unit who was flying in 1943 when he observed a 'foo fighter'. It came up underneath him in the flak over a German city. He took several shell hits which ripped gigantic holes in the fuselage, but his aircraft could still be flown. To his complete amazement and the panic of the crew within, a twelve-inch diameter glowing disc entered one large hole, flew up and down inside the fuselage and then exited harmlessly out of another hole, flying wing on him for several miles before departing upwards. One wonders whether the next day on some alien TV network, the best newsflashes from Earth featured a terrified air crew flying in flak over a German city.

The interest of the aliens in every facet of our civilized life and for that matter our uncivilized life, seems to have been pretty intense for a good number of years. UFOs were present in considerable numbers in the Korean War and have been reported also in Vietnam. Why they have this particular attraction towards keeping tabs on military action may well be to maintain a continual assessment of our strategic capacity with regard to outer space, or it may just be a purely intellectual curiosity; a kind of cosmic diary to which one day in the long distant future we may be able to refer and view some kind of video tape of our previous history.

Major Donald E. Keyhoe, United States Air Force Retired, reveals in his book *Aliens from Space** that the United States Intelligence services both within the Air Force and CIA have been gravely concerned for many years about surveillance of us by UFOs. According to Keyhoe and others, as early as 1953 the USA detected two huge space stations circling the planet in an equatorial orbit. Their size was incredible and they were situated at an earth altitude of 400 and 600 nautical miles. A cover story that they were 'natural moons' was given to the press at the time, but apparently experts of the day considered that the 'natural origin' explanation was inconsistent with the arrival of the objects in a perfectly stable and circular orbit around the earth.

Both superpowers in the world know that they are being observed by alien eyes. They also know that they can do absolutely nothing about it. The United States and the Russians have launched missiles and interceptors against the UFOs. Other than on the very rare occasion this has been totally fruitless, except to drive away the intruder – who returns another day. I suppose to achieve that alone is something, but the fact that the UFOs have often flipped around behind the intercepting jets and played cat and mouse tag with them over hundreds of miles of airspace before the jets eventually ran out of fuel indicates that our present-day military capacity in no way matches this alien superiority.

It seems to me that for far too long we have worried about the potential hostilities of the UFOs and wasted the majority of our chances of learning about their real motives. The fact that they are from a more advanced, technically superior civilization should not in itself worry us. For over thirty years now these objects have been in our skies in numbers far greater than the public is ever allowed to know. So far

*Published in the UK in 1975 by Panther Books.

there is no evidence to show deliberate harm originating from their presence; no invasion, no attack. I fail to see that another civilization or culture bent on aggression, colonization, or exploitation of this planet to their own needs should fool around for over thirty years, losing the element of surprise and initiative while our technology grows from strength to strength.

The general public now realize, in the main, that there is something behind the UFOs. Fifty-one per cent of the American public already accept them as a tangible reality and 45 per cent of the United Kingdom public took the same attitude when a survey was made in 1976.

Governments internationally should attempt to prepare for a public realization that, despite all dogmatic statements to the contrary, this planet is not alone. It is obvious from the UFOs' surveillance of every aspect of our lives, that the alien intelligence in the sky is keeping a very, very careful watch on us. Whether this is entirely from the point of view that we are a rising culture and will eventually travel the stars, or is a kind of advanced sociological and intelligence study programme is an open question. It raises the thought that if a genuine benevolent interest in our welfare from an alien culture has occurred, how do we handle it?

10

Eyes in the Sky

1977 had been a full and packed year for UFO sightings. They continued to be reported up until the very last days. On 30 December 1977 another sighting had occurred at Crymych Dyfed, West Wales. In answer to a newspaper appeal Mrs M. B. Rees wrote to me:

Dear Sir,

With reference to your request in the *Western Mail* on the 30 December 1977 I wish to inform you that my 10-year-old daughter Linda Rees and her friend Heather Morgan aged 11, sighted a strange object flying across the sky. This occurred when they were on their way to see a pet donkey at a nearby farm at about 4.30 p.m.

They were very frightened by what they had seen and heard and they rushed home to describe the mysterious object to their parents. I enclose a picture of the girls pointing towards where they had seen the whistling object. I hope that this information will be of interest to you.

But there was nothing magical about the change of the old year to the new. In 1978 events continued with equal intensity. We have already mentioned the strange weather and the return of the 'giants' in February while in other places similar alarming events were taking place with almost monotonous regularity.

On 2 January a strange spacesuited figure was seen at Rainford, near Kirby by motorists late at night, and on 17 March 1978 at 11.45 p.m. another vital incident happened. This occurred just four days after the royal premiere in London of the film *Close Encounters of the Third Kind*.

At Warrington, Cheshire, a 7-ft-tall 'giant' had been seen, wearing the typical silver spacesuit. The sighting was reported by engineer Ken Edwards at the Risley Atomic Energy Research Establishment. He had seen the incredible figure walk straight through a 10-ft-high security fence near the Manchester University Reactor and the British Nuclear Fuels Centre.

He stated: 'It was too incredible to be true. People will say I was drunk or that it was a practical joke. But I swear it was a man from space. There is no other logical explanation.'

Ken had been travelling around outside the boundary security fence when, as he described, 'I picked up a silver object in my car's headlights. It was stooped over and very

149

stiff-legged. It had a head, two arms and two legs, but the arms seemed to be coming from the chest and not the shoulders. There were two beams of light for eyes. I can't believe it but I saw it walk through the fence of the nuclear research place.' At the same time a huge power overload burnt out most of the capacitors and all of the transmitting diode circuit in Ken's mobile two-way radio fitted in his service van.

Police who took the report seriously stated that they were investigating, but came up with no conclusions. It does seem questionable with regard to the detailed description of the figure as to whether in this particular instance we were dealing with a man or with some android, equipped for ground reconnaissance and endowed with some magical property for dealing with fences; but these factors and other similarities had occurred in the 'Welsh Triangle' where Stephen Taylor had seen a similar figure outside the American base, if on that occasion of biological origin. Pauline Coombs, her young children and other witnesses had earlier observed the curious acrobatic feats of these apparently power-assisted astronauts, or were we to assume that they were members of the KGB athletics team in fancy dress?

For example, in May 1977 a sixty-four-year-old Milford Haven man had watched one of the 'giants' hovering independently over the back streets of Milford Haven for at least forty minutes. The 'astronaut', who seemed to be suspended in a kind of inanimate free fall, was seen in association with a UFO and his appearance matched the description of the other sighted figures. The witness, who wished to remain anonymous, stated that he had been wakened at 4.45 a.m. by a pulsating orange light which he found to be coming from a large, silver, egg-shaped object swinging in a pendulum-like action across a distance of 40 ft. Some considerable time elapsed and then he saw the floating 'giant' only some twenty yards away, at the same altitude as the UFO. Both UFO and 'space walker' departed slowly away over the terraced houses into the darkness, giving no clue as to what they had been surveying in such detail over this quiet Milford Haven suburb bordering the oil refinery. Rather a late hour, even for an interplanetary peeping tom, at 5.00 in the morning, although there does seem to be a definite attraction towards night surveillance in UFO activity as opposed to daylight operations.

Fortunately this had not been the case in one incident which I must refer to as it may be deeply significant to our other clues. It had occurred on 26 October 1967 over Moigne Down near Lulworth Cove in Dorset, and had been observed by Mr Angus Brooks, a retired administration officer of BOAC's Comet Flight. He had been walking his dog, an Alsatian, when he had seen in a clear sky a remarkable object descending into view, levelling out and hovering at an altitude of approximately 300 ft, only some 400 yards distant from him. The UFO, which was circular, carried four arms: one was projected ahead of the object and three were stowed behind it. When the object had come to rest and steadied itself, hovering constantly despite the strong wind, two of the rear arms deployed on either side and formed a cross-like structure. Mr Brooks's Alsatian seemed very agitated by the presence of the object as he watched it hover motionless for twenty minutes before stowing its arms yet again. Then it climbed away into the sky. The important factor involved in the sighting is, significantly, that apart from its having been reported by an excellently credible witness, the UFO had hovered in very close proximity to the Winfrith Atomic Station and the Portland Naval Base. Mr Brooks stated that the object seemed to be constructed of some kind of translucent metal and his description of the object had been backed up by other sightings of a similar mystery aerial craft over Devon, Northampton and London during the same period. (Just in passing, the Ministry of Defence's comments and 'explanations', such as 'spots in the eyes' issued at the time are hardly worthy of mention.)

Do we in this precise sighting have a clear indication of a

UFO using some kind of extensive and specialized aerial equipment? What radiations was it searching for with such an extensive antenna? Was it some kind of radiation coming from St Brides Bay and the American installations which had alerted the UFOs to take a special interest in the 'Welsh Triangle'? The intense interest in nuclear research and nuclear reactors may also give us a clue.

On 11 February 1978 in the period of strange weather, Haverfordwest near St Brides Bay was 'bombed' by some curious crystals. At 7.15 on the Saturday morning Mr Frederick Evans, aged twenty-eight, heard a shower of stones falling on the roof of his house. He stated, 'It was really pounding the roof and I just thought it was a hailstorm', but when he emerged he found that for an area of 600 yards in all directions up and down the street the ground was covered in strange quartz-like crystals which had fallen from the sky.

'They were reddish brown in colour when I picked them up, then they began to change colour. Some went light brown and others transparent. They were very hard, just like stone, and seemed to generate their own heat,' reported Mr Evans.

This sounded curiously like chemical cloud bombing and although we were never fortunate enough to recover any of the crystals, there did seem to be the possibility that some conventional aerial operation might be attempting to take some water out of the clouds or the power out of the storm. Was somebody trying to rectify adverse weather conditions produced by some unnatural means?

Back in August 1977 Terry and Sandra Marston had reported another unexplained 'meteorological' phenomenon at almost the exact location where their son Mark had formerly seen one of the 'giants'. Terry and family had gone down to a field in which they keep their pet pony, and having spent a pleasant sunny afternoon they returned to their car parked on the verge of the nearby road at Herbrandston. They found hovering over the car a rectangular cube-shaped 'cloud'. The cloud descended partly over the car, shrouding it in its misty form and Terry, fearing that his vehicle was on fire, ran to the car and opened the door. He frantically sought some source of the smoke but could find nothing amiss. However, while inside the mysterious cloud, he experienced great difficulty in breathing and became nauseated.

He remembers, 'There was a terrible smell, sulphurous; and it was very cold.' The temperature inside the cloud was quite unnatural and Terry, in his shirt sleeves, remembers his teeth chattering with the intense cold. So badly affected was he by the strange physiological effects that he had to leave the car, gasping, and sit on the verge of the road some yards away to recover his breath. At this point the curious cloud, which was not very much larger than Terry's Austin 1800 saloon, ascended a little and moved off down the verge of the road, maintaining its sharply defined outlines. At no point was a solid body visible within it but Terry felt that it could not possibly have been any kind of natural phenomenon as the day was so cloudless and no mist or fog was present in the warm summer air.

Terry has since had some electrical problems with the vehicle and whether this is directly associated with the family's experiences is not easy to determine, but it is a clearly established characteristic of UFOs that they can stop vehicles by stalling the electrics of internal combustion engines, although diesel engines seem unaffected. The fact that the method can be employed more deliberately and precisely was demonstrated in one classic air chase involving two Phantom jet fighters of the Imperial Iranian Air Force. The 'dog fight' had taken place at 10.30 p.m. on 18 September 1976, and appeared to involve an object similar to that observed by Angus Brooks over Dorset nine years previously.

Alarmed citizens phoned the local air traffic control tower, describing 'a fan with four blades'. After the fourth call the senior controller, Hossain Pirouzi, employed at

153

Tehran's Merhabad Airport for thirteen years, located the object visually with binoculars.

He stated: 'After about five minutes I saw the object, a rectangular shape about five miles away at a height of 6,000 feet and northeast of the tower. The right end was blue, the left end was blue and in the middle was a flashing red light. The object we saw was see-sawing up and down and moving towards the north.'

The controller immediately phoned the senior Iranian Air Force officer on duty, General Abdullah Azarbarzan, who launched a Phantom night fighter equipped with air-to-air radar. The aircraft kept in radio communication with ground control and General Azarbarzan stated that the UFO was described to him as 'quite circular and just like a saucer, and the shape of the cockpit was a ball – half a ball.'

The air traffic controller, Hossain Pirouzi, launched a second aircraft and ordered the first jet to close up on the object but the pilot reported: 'I'm going to Mach 2 [about 1,400 miles an hour] and I'm fifty miles behind the object. I can't catch him.'

From then on, Pirouzi stated, the Phantoms were chasing the object all over the place to the north and west with the UFO showing fantastic speed and seeming to disappear then reappear. At one point when the pilot was pursuing the UFO it suddenly performed an amazing manoeuvre and an alarmed pilot communicated to the ground: 'It's about twenty miles behind. It's following me! Oh! now . . .', as the radio went dead.

The Phantom now came within visual sight of the tower and zoomed low over the field, watched by amazed controllers who could see the brilliantly illuminated rectangular UFO virtually on top of the aircraft, sitting above its tailplane. Observers stated that the unidentified object appeared to be dark and sort of rectangular shaped, seen from their angle, with brilliant lights.

Throughout five and a half hours two Phantoms were involved: the one sent up first was followed by a replacement when it ran low on fuel. At various times and some-times just prior to an attempted attack, the UFO at a distance of fifteen miles would suddenly nullify all of the Phantoms' electronics and the aircraft would find themselves electrically dead.

General Azarbarzan stated, 'That happened to three different planes. We had two fighters – that happened to both of them – and one airliner, which was flying in the area at the time. This technology they [the UFOs] were using was something we haven't had before, and we don't have it. It was extremely strange and unexplainable.'

The UFO seemed capable of jamming any electrical system on the Phantoms whenever the aircraft approached too close. It also had the capacity not only to outmanoeuvre the jet fighters but to flip around behind them and stick on their tails despite all evasive actions. At no point was the Iranian Air Force capable of launching an attack on the UFO, as the electronic failures successfully jammed weapons systems and communication electronics.

Just after 4 a.m. on the 19th, the UFO climbed away and left the area but it was apparently sighted only forty-five minutes later, some 3,200 miles to the west, by a TAP Boeing 707 leaving Lisbon. The UFO, which matched the Iranian description, flashed across the course of the airliner and was reported as a 'near miss' by the crew. To cover this distance the craft must have averaged an air speed of approximately 4,267 miles per hour.

One curious item of information is that as long ago as 1845 a UFO was sighted in the same area north of Madeira Island and west of Lisbon, submerging in the sea. It is always possible of course that we have underestimated the duration of time that the UFOs have been here and that possibly they have had established facilities under the surface of the ocean. By way of coincidence I also have two other sightings of UFOs travelling along the identical route from Tehran to Lisbon. One occurred over Sicily in 1845 and the other over the Ionian Sea in 1853.

Some writers have speculated that the UFOs never really left the Earth but that their presence here is continuous, if variable in numbers and intensity. It could well be that some permanent facility has existed on this planet since their initial interest here, possibly many millennia ago.

The question stands unanswered as to why the UFO over Tehran found it necessary to maintain its position while outmanoeuvring the Phantom jets for over five and a half hours, whereas in all other instances it is the general practice for UFOs to make off when intercepted. Perhaps significant is the observation by one of the pilots that the UFO at one point appeared to break in two and that one of the luminous objects descended to the ground.* This happened shortly before the principal UFO departed from the area, and although no trace was ever found of the object which had come down, it seems likely that some kind of rendezvous was planned which was so important that it could not be cancelled or interfered with by the unwelcome intervention of the Imperial Iranian Air Force.

As opposed to the security job done by terrestrial governments and air forces, the alien intelligence has remained throughout the years almost completely inscrutable.

We should not for one moment take a complacent attitude that the UFO situation is nothing to do with us, that it is a disconnected area of inquiry and activity which is beyond human ken and as insignificant as the social customs of a lost African tribe. For this very attitude adopted by some major governments is a dangerous apathy, politically ill-advised and strategically vulnerable.

The effects of alien culture on our human twentieth-century civilization could, I am convinced, be a startling reality by the twenty-first century!

---

* Ground-based witnesses observed the landing of this craft and subsequent investigation showed it had rested on three legs, and had been 4·5 metres in diameter and weighed 5 tons.

11

Clones, Cars and Cosmonauts

The clandestine landing of UFOs in remote places is not an unusual occurrence. One such event took place in late 1976 on the edge of the thinly populated natural wilderness of Dartmoor in the West of England. Mr John Perrot was in his car parked near the granite landmark of Haytor late at night, when he was surprised by the low-level arrival of a 30-ft-diameter disc-shaped UFO. The UFO, which passed low over his unlit vehicle, was on an approach path for a landing in the valley below. Mr Perrot, unnerved by the experience, drove away from the area at high speed but stopped farther down the valley long enough to observe that the machine had landed near the roadside and that a diminutive humanoid figure had emerged from the craft, carrying a torchlight-like device. The witness was not inclined to investigate the situation in this deserted and darkened area of unspoilt Britain and left the scene none the wiser as to the purpose of the ufonaut's mission.

Other reports had come from the same desolate area. A postman, Mr H. Goldsworthy, recalled an earlier dawn experience: 'I was going to work one morning at 5.50; I saw a bright light in the sky which at first I thought was a star, but I realized that it was coming towards me. I stopped and then as it came nearer I saw it had flashing lights, about four. It eventually passed overhead and headed towards the moors. I know by the shape it was not an aeroplane, and there was no sound. I was in the RAF during the war and estimate that it was at about 5,000 or 6,000 feet.'

A daylight sighting followed, three months later. An anonymous woman witness stated: 'My friend and I sighted a strange object in the sky. My friend happened to look into the sky. For about four minutes we watched this strange object drift across then ascend until it was out of sight. We reported it to a policeman at about 1 p.m. He took my name and address and said that if any more strange accounts were reported that afternoon, they would get in touch with me. We saw the object again later on. Two jets were flying at the same height as the object. It seemed to glide across the sky not as fast as a jet, though it went up very quickly. We have tried to explain it with logic but have found it impossible. The police came to my home that evening and seemed very interested.'

Further reports came in around the same period, including the description of 'a silver, motionless, oblong object' seen in daylight by a driver on the Bere Alston Road at Gunnislake. A jet aircraft was seen in the sky at the same time and both the object and the plane passed out of sight behind trees. Two other people, while driving in their car on a nearby highway, saw a large glowing object which stopped then continued to hover over the road very close to them; while a courting couple in Haytor car park were frightened by a low-level UFO with two red flashing lights. The object passed low over them and continued towards the south coast. The area where the sightings had been reported lies just across the Bristol Channel from the Pembrokeshire coastline and the 'Welsh Triangle'.

Right up to the completion of the manuscript of this book, UFOs were continuing to be seen on a regular basis. One such was reported on 25 July 1978 over Chepstow racecourse. The principal witness, Mr Tony Rostenburg, thirty-two-year-old managing director of a catering firm, was staying overnight together with his staff at the racecourse in preparation for the weekend's 'Chepstow Spectacular Show'. It was early morning and Mr Rostenburg was the first up. He described his experience: 'I saw this thing, so I decided to get the others to take a look at it. It was just like a ball with three lights on it. I could see it distinctly as it moved sideways up and down and it was spinning clearly. There is no way an aircraft could have looked or moved like that.'

The UFO hovered over the course for five minutes while Mr Rostenburg aroused the other members of staff, and they also witnessed the strange, spinning saucer. Fifteen-year-old Stuart Denks said: 'Seeing is believing. It was real and pretty frightening.'

Finally the UFO took off and vanished at high speed up into the clouds.

In May 1978 a red, ball-like UFO had frightened swimmers and holidaymakers one sunny afternoon at St Brides Haven, a sheltered cove one mile from Ripperston Farm. The sphere, which appeared flying low along the coast from the direction of Stack Rocks, caused bathers to run from the water and visitors to desert the beach in panic.

In the same month another bright, star-like UFO hovered late at night over the milking complex near to the Coombs's farmhouse.

Many times it has been asked, 'Why do not the UFOs land openly?' The reasons are apparent from a simple and informed examination of the history of the subject. An extensive analysis of the United States Air Force policy towards the strange alien vessels has revealed an alarming situation. From an initial disbelief in their existence the US Intelligence services quickly realized that the phenomena were real and likely to be intelligently controlled machines from outer space. Some early contact attempts indicated that they were controlled by people not too unlike ourselves but maybe sufficiently different to cause some public alarm. One must remember that the years of the early 1950s were just after the Second World War, and the American administration was nervous over its world position and the territorial ambitions of an unnamed foreign power, which for the sake of argument we shall call Russia. In this atmosphere it was almost impossible for the military authorities or the president, if indeed he was fully acquainted with the situation, to go to the people and declare the real situation. In a country which had only recently achieved peace after a tragically costly war, how could a government tell the people that they were being surveyed by aerial craft over which they had no control and which displayed a technology that they could not match?

To the military-minded generals, the fruit that the superior UFOs held out to them was irresistible. They were concerned only with thoughts of capturing such a machine in order that they might duplicate its mechanics and thereby insure world security or at least their own nation's security, by duplicating an aerial armada of these vessels which would insure the safety of the United States for all time against overseas aggressors. It was with these motives that, at various times, orders were issued that UFOs were to be captured at all costs. The long-term and interplanetary repercussions of this policy seemed to be completely missed by Intelligence and Air Force chiefs not only in the United States but in other air forces attempting this kind of technical coup. Needless to say, none of the interception attempts were successful, although it is thought that at least one UFO was destroyed by the direct hit of a missile. This apparently was launched from a United States vessel in the South Atlantic in 1963, a panic measure when the Navy Department took the situation into its own hands, fearing that the ship was in danger. It must have taken the UFO completely by surprise, for the missile, which was fired from a range of four miles, connected while the alien craft was still hovering, and the result was a terrific explosion; but it produced only thousands of pieces which promptly sank to the ocean floor and were never recovered. After the early attempts of the 1950s to 1960s and 'dog-fights' with various national air forces, the UFOs became very cautious and made a point of outmanoeuvring all likely interceptors.

It was also after the early days that it was noticeable that the alien craft copied anti-collision beacons, as there had previously been several records of mid-air collisions involving UFOs and commercial aircraft, in at least two cases with fatal results. There seems no reason to believe that these were anything more than accidents, although much play has been

160

made of them by some sensational writers. Over the years the alien craft seem to have improved in their performance and new designs have been introduced. The original craft were all saucer- or torpedo-shaped but, later, aircraft pilots reported egg-shaped vehicles and a greater use of smaller, apparently remotely controlled discs. Similarly, the number of landings increased and where these were in areas of some hazard the use of various forms of 'robots' seemed favoured. This again was hardly surprising as by the mid 1960s UFOs while landed had been fired at on numerous occasions by various individuals, both military and civilian, using small-arms, rifles and machine-guns. There had apparently been a few hits on ufonauts who sometimes had landed unsuspectingly on the outskirts of remote towns in North and South America only to find their presence produced hysteria and panic, bringing fire from anybody around with some kind of weapon. Naturally none of these occurrences has improved the prospects of open contact being established.

The methods employed by the alien intelligence in defence of military actions seem to be a mixture of high-grade technology and psychological distraction. When engaged in some ground operation which has been disturbed by innocent bystanders stumbling across a landed craft, they seem to have used on occasions a method of paralysation which affects the witnesses for a few hours or may induce temporary unconsciousness. In quite a number of cases some kind of 'mirage' seems to have been produced, frightening enough to the unwanted intruder who quickly departs to the nearest newspaper declaring that monsters from outer space have landed. Unnerving human beings seems to be the favourite method of losing the unwanted interest rather than a direct physical confrontation. Certainly the ufonauts seem to have every reason to suspect terrestrial motives and human character. For as it has been presented to them so far, it is not a very encouraging or attractive aspect of ourselves as a species and seems to have brought about various miscalculations on the part of the ufonauts, leading to an

161

extreme cautiousness towards our culture and a definite apprehension about making contact.

There is one general area of communication which is the exception to their rule, and seems to be recognized as such by the alien intelligence. This is the phenomenally high number of sightings and close encounters by children. The aliens obviously realize that children present little or no threat to them, as they have often approached each other with no preconceived instincts of fear. Hence one finds that as opposed to an adult situation, which is treated in a very cautious and defensive manner, the aliens often approach children, or are seen in close proximity to groups of children, apparently either completely oblivious to their presence or taking an engaging interest in their activities. Citing just a few examples will clearly demonstrate this point.

On 7 February 1977 Billy Price wrote to me: 'In Penarth, Cardiff on Tuesday, February 2nd between 9.15 and 9.30 p.m., I and several other boys saw a white light moving about 10 ft from the ground. It was moving at a very high speed. As far as we could see it was cigar-shaped and some think that they saw a reddish tint to it. We saw it moving in different directions also at a very high speed. As some other boys from a nearby school saw a similar object on the following evening we would be interested to know if you could explain it, and also if you have received any similar reports.'

On 4 February 1977 a group of twenty children at Hubberston School, Milford Haven sighted a cigar-shaped UFO hovering overhead during their lunch break. Significantly this was on the same day as the children at Broad Haven saw a UFO land in the field near to their primary school, as I have already reported in detail in chapter 1.

One week later, on 11 February, nine girls and their teacher at Rhosybol School, Anglesey also saw a cigar-shaped object hovering over the school in good visibility that sunny afternoon; and on 16 February Graham Howells, aged thirteen, of Pembroke Dock sighted a bright silver metallic object hovering over the Pembroke School as he arrived early on the Wednesday morning.

He reported: 'It had a dome in the middle which was dark grey most of the time but flashed to a dazzling white about every five seconds. It resembled a plate with a burnt fried egg on it. Around the rim of the "plate" it had greeny-yellowish lights and what seemed to be retrorockets. The plate seemed to be revolving as well. Looking at the whole thing from the side it would probably appear cigar-shaped. Even though it was foggy, I'm sure it wasn't a helicopter or a weather balloon because it stayed completely still all of the time I was looking at it. It couldn't have been smoke from the power station because it flashed and I had quite a good view of the thing.'

The following day, 17 February, Mark Jones, a twelve-year-old Haverfordwest schoolboy, together with his friend Llewellyn Edwards, also twelve, sighted a UFO hovering near the Haverfordwest Grammar School. The boys, who observed the object from a distance of about 40 yards, said that it was a 15-foot-long, orange cigar-shaped fuselage, carrying a blue flashing light. They lobbed a stone at it and it took off at high speed and vanished. They were rather unnerved by the experience and ran all the way to the police station, where they reported the incident. Mark recalls: 'The police drove us back to the field, but they couldn't find any sign of it.' This was the second time that Mark Jones had made an observation of a UFO within a two-month period.

Later in the year Mr P. D. May of Aberdare wrote to me: 'I have been prompted to write to you after reading the article in the *Western Mail* on 30 December regarding UFOs seen in Wales. On Monday, 31 October 1977 at approximately 7.15 p.m. my sons Simon and Richard came running into the house saying they had seen a UFO. As they were playing with other children that night they saw the object moving slowly towards them and continuing on in the direction of Glynneath. It made no sound at all as it passed overhead. Simon drew a sketch of what he saw that night, a copy of which is enclosed. Simon has drawn this sketch himself but the written details have been entered by me on his instructions. A few nights before this incident my wife and myself together with my brother-in-law and sister-in-law also saw what we thought was a "strange object" in the sky. There was no sound at all but the object seemed to be at a greater distance away from us than it was from the children. The object we saw also had a red flashing light and the white light was a very brilliant light. It moved fairly slowly and was on a circular course. Hoping this information will be of some help.'

The sketches provided by Mr May and drawn by his nine- and eight-year-old sons Simon and Richard shows a circular object having nineteen small white lights around the rim, with three very bright white lights towards the rear of the object underneath, and a slowly pulsating single red light off centre towards the front of the object positioned in the direction of travel.

Pembroke was the scene of another sighting on 28 November of the same year. Brian Harnikel, aged fifteen, and his fourteen-year-old sister Catherine were walking across Orange Gardens just after 10 p.m. when they sighted a dome-like object in the sky, also carrying three white lights.

Brian stated: 'The object was making its way very slowly in the direction of Freshwater East. It wasn't making any noise and to gauge the size I took a penny out of my pocket and held it at arm's length. It covered the UFO, which was at a great height, completely.' Brian ran home to tell his brother Paul and together they watched the UFO for about thirty seconds until it went out of sight. They got in touch with the police and later two policemen called on them for further details. Again, this was the second time that these children had sighted a UFO, for together with their mother they had attempted earlier in the year to take photographs of an unidentified object which they had all seen making its way across the sky at a relatively low altitude. Regrettably the photography was unsuccessful.

It seemed fairly obvious from the continuous train of reports that Welsh schools were being systematically surveyed by the alien intelligence. Earlier in the year, during February, at the height of the general excitement, Katrina and Kieron Coombs together with other children had independently seen UFOs hovering over the Milford Haven Comprehensive School.

On one occasion two or three of the pupils had been mysteriously affected by unusual stomach cramps after the sighting and had had to receive attention from the school nurse. It is difficult to say whether this physiological effect was a direct result of the low passing of the UFO, but one can only note the coincidence.

English schools had apparently been surveyed previously, as was evidenced by a train of reports from St Hugh's School, Woodhall Spa, Lincs, the witnesses being Mark Tinsley and his friend James who reported UFOs landing in a nearby wood called Ostlers' Plantation; and an earlier report from three adults and ninety schoolchildren at Treleigh Comprehensive School, Redruth. The reported object, which had been high in the midday sky and seen during excellent visibility, was described as 'resembling two dinner plates face to face'.

One of the teachers, Miss Deborah Foster, said, 'It was white and spinning. It appeared to be very high up and came from the Truro direction. We lost sight of it over Carn Brey. It was saucer-shaped and seemed to have an aura or halo.'

Mr Sam Hawkins, another teacher, saw silver and yellow flashes coming from the object, which was travelling very slowly, and he stated: 'It went through high cloud yet we could still see it.'

The school secretary, Sylvia Harris, confirmed the flashes and the description of the object. She remembers: 'They were like lightning and were spasmodic. I have never seen anything like it before. It was a little frightening. I do not like anything I cannot explain.'

The pupils confirmed that the object appeared to be a sphere, spinning, emitting flashes, that it bore no markings and seemed to change to a green hue when behind high clouds. Mr Sidney Thorne, the headmaster, discounted suggestions that it may have been a weather balloon as apparently the object had performed a distinct manoeuvre. He further stated that other UFOs had been seen earlier by parents at a school north of Redruth.

Schoolchildren were not the only people to be observing UFOs in considerable quantity. Mr D. J. Palmer wrote to me: 'I am an amateur astronomer and at the age of thirty during astronomical observations I have no less than seven definite UFO sightings to my credit, from disc-shaped objects in formation to star-like objects pulsating and changing colour.'

Another astronomer, Mr W. G. Eales, wrote: 'November 1976, 10.30 p.m., late in the month, broken cloud . . . gazing into the heavens, there appeared two red discs; now they were not brilliant red, more of a glow. They were about 3 inches in diameter, spaced about a foot apart (apparently), travelling from S.S.W. to N.N.E. direction. I did not see them coming towards me but observed them spontaneously, slightly to the right of my forward vision.

'The time of sighting and leaving my vision was no more than 9 to 10 seconds, disappearing over the rooftops at a reasonable speed and at what height I am at a loss to say. It was a dark night, but I can say that they were below the cloud ceiling.

'The night was quiet, and I saw two glowing discs moving across the heavens silently, no hum, no rushing sound as of wind, in complete silence, being held in a horizontal position, by what? Was there a solid body between them, who knows?

'It has puzzled me much, one thing I am sorry about, and that is, I have night glasses and five-inch spectroscope, but owing to it not being a good night for stargazing they were not at hand. Who is ever prepared when strange things ever occur?'

At the same time a Mrs Ramsier wrote to me of an amusing incident in Ireland which emphasizes the reluctance of the UFOs to land. She described: 'It was where I was born, Miltown Molbay, Co. Clare. It was like a great big ball of fire, it landed in the middle of our garden. The time would be about 10 o'clock at night. I was very frightened and ran indoors. There were several men having a game of cards, they went out of the back door and went into the shed for forks, shovels and sticks – as they got near, it lifted off, no engines, no noise, and they followed it for about a mile across the fields; when it came to the cemetery it went on over the wall; they came back. Next morning there were no marks, no sign of anything having landed. This is a true story but of course no one would believe it.'

With so much UFO activity over the years one wonders if any of the alien craft has ever made a forced landing, or crashed. The answer most definitely seems to be in the affirmative, as many times UFOs have been seen grounded, with their operators working outside on the hull or on some mechanism needing repair. This is one of the consistent cases where the intrusion of would-be witnesses is delayed by the aliens' favourite mechanism, the paralyzing ray, which usually knocks the witness flat on his back, leaving him conscious but immobile, until the UFO has safely taken off. Whether in fact any of the world governments has ever succeeded in capturing a crashed UFO is a matter of considerable speculation and high secrecy. However, it seems possible that one report from the island of Spitzbergen may have some foundation of truth in it. Norwegian military pilots had observed wreckage on the island and as it was thought to be that of a crashed aircraft, a rescue team was dispatched. What they found was apparently no terrestrial machine but the remnants of a crashed UFO. Considerable secrecy and 'explanations' surrounded the mystery but the chairman of the board of inquiry, Colonel Gernod Darnbyl, stated: 'Some time ago a misunderstanding was caused by saying that this disc was of Soviet origin. It has – this we wish to state emphatically – not been built by any country on Earth. The materials used in its construction are completely unknown to all experts who participated in the investigation.'

Although the story made some headlines in the Norwegian press during the mid 1950s, after consultations with US and British Government authorities the story was submerged into complete secrecy to the point at which an inquiry to the Norwegian authorities brought only: 'I regret that it is impossible for me to respond to your questions at this time', from a spokesman who declined either to confirm or deny the story.

One thing is certain: fragments of UFOs have been retrieved. Some of them have found their way into government laboratories. The purity of the metals analysed suggests a use of superconductors, as with the decrease in the percentage of unwanted trace elements the conductivity of pure metals increases dramatically.

Fragments of UFOs have to my knowledge been recovered from various countries in Scandinavia, North and South America and France and appear to be small breakages that have fallen from UFOs due to either minor damage on landing or to overheating in the propulsion system. I have myself seen a piece recovered by British investigators which appeared to be good old-fashioned aluminium. Everything that I have come across still confirms me in my assertion that the UFOs are solid machines flown by flesh-and-blood operators. I think that it is only the advanced element of the technology which appears to give them their supernatural or ghostly qualities. It is very easy to dismiss the phenomena under the convenient heading of 'psychic', in order to diminish its importance or disregard its relevance to science and society. But I have yet to find a ghost who has successfully burnt circular patches on green grass, left radiation traces or bent steel brackets on overhead power pylons.

One fascinating story of a grounded UFO comes from behind the Iron Curtain, therefore I am not in a position to check out its details, but it warrants an inclusion here as a significant case which will lend detail to our next chapter in which the most revealing information on the ufonauts emerges from cases within the 'Triangle'. The incident allegedly occurred during the month of January, a few years ago, at Gdynia (Gdansk), Poland.

A strange object was seen to fall into the harbour, and a man was found wandering along the seashore in an extremely confused state. He was taken to a local medical clinic for observation and it was discovered that he had an unusual number of fingers. (Whether more or less than normal, is unclear.) He was dressed in a onepiece suit which defied all efforts at removing it. Eventually it was cut away with the aid of metal shears and found to consist of exceptionally tough multi-layered material. A metal 'bracelet' on one of his wrists was removed, after which he immediately died. A post-mortem examination revealed significant differences in the arrangement of his internal organs and circulatory system, which was reported to have followed a spiral path around his body.

Without warning the hospital was suddenly sealed off by the Polish authorities, who placed guards at the entrance. No one was allowed in or out of the bay where the corpse was lying. Shortly afterwards a lorry arrived, complete with refrigerated container, and very heavily guarded. The corpse was put on board. The strange cargo then departed to a secret research institute in Moscow from which no further news ever emerged.

The story, which was at first thought to be a rather wild rumour, was unexpectedly confirmed by a Polish *émigré* living in London who claimed that he had been on the staff of the Gdynia hospital at the time and that all the details of the story were correct.

If the account is true, we can assume that the alien 'astronaut' was working under some degree of unnatural stress in our atmosphere and that he was protected by his suit and possibly assisted by some form of 'pacer' incorporated in the 'bracelet'. The removal of these life-support system aids might have caused his sudden and premature death and it is to be regretted that no more information is available about the alleged incident. The fact that nothing was said by the USSR authorities is of course no surprise.

From this and other reports, of which I myself have studied over 300, it seems that the ufonauts, in physical characteristics, are very similar to human beings; that is, they have two legs, two arms and a head and they stand in the normal upright position as we do. It would also seem, from the great variety of information available on the subject, that we are being visited from various origins of interplanetary life some of whom can breathe in our atmosphere. Individuals are variously described as being from 3 ft 6 in up to 12 ft tall, with the predominance being towards the lower heights. Again this does not unduly surprise me as here on planet Earth, even with one continent, Africa, we find a great variation in normal stature. For example, the tall Masai, many of them over 7 ft, in comparison with the diminutive pygmies of the dense jungle forest give an adequate example of anthropological variation and adaptation to the conditions within one relatively small area, a matter of a few hundred miles. So why should we be surprised when operators of craft from elsewhere have similar variations in height? Even our 'giants' of the 'Welsh Triangle' were hardly any higher than some members of the Harlem Globetrotters' basketball team.

There are a few reports of 'monsters', but upon deeper examination even these tend to lose their more Frankensteinish aspects. Under conditions of stress, descriptions by a witness can often be exaggerated, especially when they are being prompted by reporters looking for an emphasis on the scary and weird. Generally speaking, one finds when talking to the witnesses personally that the grotesque cartoonlike pictures produced from their descriptions bear a poor resemblance to the individuals in question. I do not say that on occasions the UFO operators may not have induced or produced a hologram of some rather weird-looking fictional creature in order simply to scare off unwanted 'guests'.

The equipment worn by the operators over the years seems to vary from completely hermetically sealed spacesuits, similar to those supplied to the American astronauts, to the kind of 'ski-suit' protective clothing apparently used by the unfortunate ufonaut who crashed in Poland. In both cases it would seem that air pressure is not a problem and even the possibility that the ufonauts can in fact completely adapt, but perhaps for only short periods of time, was evidenced by one of the most revealing incidents of the whole saga of the 'Welsh Triangle'. The events which, upon our request, were kept confidential by the witnesses, occurred earlier in the year of 1977. I deal with them at this point because it is important to bring them into consideration in relation to other significant information.

After the dramatic teleportation of Billy Coombs's herd of cows two more teleportations took place. At one of these I myself was present. Both Jane and I were at the farmhouse one night, together with Clive Harold. The cows were safely locked up in their steel-gated milking complex and the night was blustery and dark. Clive left for London at about 11.30 p.m. and Jane and I were about to take our leave when Clinton came running in to the sitting-room to say that the cows had broken out and were in an adjoining paddock. We all rushed down to the complex, together with the other members of the family, to assist in herding them back. But Billy was perplexed to find that none of the safety bolts on the covered yard gates were out of place and that no gates were open. Somehow the cows had negotiated the distance between the covered yard and the paddock without displacement of any of the steel fences or opening any of the gates. The incident remained inexplicable.

It was earlier on this same evening that the Coombs family had confided their most startling encounter. The incident

171

had occurred at about the time of the previous teleportation of the cows and after the main series of events which had taken place. Pauline had gone to market with the younger children to collect the week's shopping and was returning somewhere back along the road between Haverfordwest and St Brides. Clinton was alone in the farmhouse and in the adjoining cottage, Caroline Class, the wife of another farmworker, was busy in her kitchen. Both Clinton and Caroline were independently aware of some movement on the track which runs by the houses and outside they could see over the top of the three-foot-high stone garden wall what they took to be the roof of a large and 'futuristic' sports car. It was extremely large, and gently dome-shaped on the top which was surrounded by tinted curved glass. To the front and rear was a curved flange. It was rectangular and had wheels.

Caroline could see one individual sitting in the car and another individual wandering about down by the milking complex and apparently inspecting it. Although not usually a nervous person Caroline, an attractive girl in her mid twenties, was very unnerved by the appearance of the 'visitors' and their vehicle. Both of them were dressed in grey-blue two-piece suits without hats and were exceptionally tall, the man down by the farmbuildings having fairer hair than the man in the 'car' whose hair was darker.

Visitors to the farm were relatively uncommon and Caroline wondered what the gentlemen wanted. She went to the front door and looked down towards the farming complex where one of the visitors was still walking about. Now the farming complex is about 100 yards away downhill over the muddy, potholed track and it was therefore with considerable surprise that Caroline, having peeked at the visitor and turned to come into the house, took a couple of paces and suddenly found that he was now behind her. How could he possibly have covered that distance in a second or two?

He addressed her in accented English: 'Where is Mrs Pauline Coombs?'

Caroline tried to answer calmly although she was un-nerved by the stranger's appearance, apparent speed of foot, and his question. The date was 6 June 1977 and up to this time Pauline had not featured largely in newspaper articles or publications, so how did the stranger know that Caroline was not Pauline Coombs? How did he know that she was not at home when he had not even been to Pauline's house yet? The distance that he had travelled, arriving soundlessly and not out of breath, was incredible. His appearance was not unhuman but sufficiently different for Caroline to feel uneasy. His forehead was exceptionally high and his hair was swept straight back over his head. He had a pointed chin and particularly large, penetrating blue eyes which seemed to go right through her and examine her thoughts. His English was flawless, but not as flowing as in the case of somebody speaking his native tongue; and definitely 'foreign', although she could not place the linguistic pronunciation it resembled. His clothes were of exceptionally fine texture and quality, immaculately pressed and his shoes were polished. He definitely was not 'from the country' and yet he seemed to know about the people he had come to see. He pressed Caroline for further information as to when Pauline would return.

His companion sat motionless in the 'car', looking straight ahead and giving no sign of his thoughts or reactions. Caroline was particularly struck by the remarkable similarity of the two figures. Indeed she would have sworn that they were identical twins. Only their clothes were slightly different. One of the suits, although of the same style as the second, was somewhat greyer in material than the other, which was a deeper blue. The stranger produced a detailed map of the area and requested Caroline to show him exactly where he was. This she did and answered his questions on the proximity of the local town and the surroundings. He also inquired whether any UFO sightings had been reported in the area and Caroline informed him that the children of the Broad Haven Primary School had sighted something in

173

the field adjoining. Curiously Caroline felt that the stranger anticipated her answers before she could get them out.

He also expressed an urgency to return to some kind of rendezvous at Croesgoch, a small village directly across St Brides Bay on a line from Ripperston Farm to the small cove of Mill Haven opposite Stack Rocks. By way of co-incidence, in early April 1977 a Mr Smith on holiday from Anglesey had observed from Croesgoch a huge spaceship hovering about 600 ft above the ground. He had described it as 'a golden, pencil-shaped light at an angle in the sky with what looked like a snout at the top end. Underneath was another patch of light, more rounded.' Mr Smith estimated that the 'mother ship' was approximately one mile distant from him and of immense proportions. (In earlier years the United States Air Force had also observed these carrier craft and estimated some of them to be in excess of 2,000 ft long overall.)

Caroline felt that she had not been of much help to her other-worldly visitor and silently hoped he would leave. Barely had the thought passed through her mind when the stranger courteously departed and walked towards the Coombs's farmhouse next door.

All this was being observed by Clinton who was hiding behind the curtains at the upstairs window overlooking the road. Clinton is not a nervous person either, and therefore his reactions now were particularly out of character, for upon seeing the strangers approaching he immediately rushed downstairs to the front door and bolted it and then went quickly to the rear of the house to make the kitchen door secure as well. Why he did this he later could not really explain; he had just acted instinctively. He was so frightened by the visitors' appearance that he could not even face them and he returned hurriedly to the upstairs window to observe their departure. They knocked at the door, waited a moment or two, then returned to their vehicle. Very quickly the 'car' moved forward up the lane leaving the farm and was out of sight within a few seconds. Clinton was relieved to see

Pauline's car with the children on board arrive from market down the same track, only two seconds after the strangers had departed. He went cautiously to the front door to tell his mother of the strange encounter.

Clinton opened the door. 'Did you see the car?' he inquired excitedly. Pauline looked at him as if he were slightly deranged. 'What car?' she asked incredulously. For she had seen no car at all. Now the lane that goes from Ripperston Farm is a dirt road bounded by thick, 8 foot-high banks and hedges. Other than making a sharp turn near the house, it is dead straight for approximately half a mile and it is practically impossible for two cars to pass, and certainly impossible for them to pass each other unnoticed. But Pauline had seen nothing, nothing at all. No car, no strangers; and yet Clinton had watched the car enter the lane only two or three seconds before Pauline had arrived from the opposite direction around the corner. How had this phenomenal trick been produced? How could the car have instantly disappeared? Furthermore it had departed in complete silence. No engine noise, no crunching of gravel under the heavy-looking bodywork. It had just glided away!

Shortly afterwards it was to appear again. Pretty Francine Granville was sitting writing in the lounge of the Haven Fort Hotel. She often took this position as it gave her an unrestricted view over the front of the hotel drive and car park and as her mother was out shopping it allowed her quickly to observe any new arrivals. Francine is an experienced receptionist and has dealt with hundreds of visitors, therefore she is not in the least perturbed by people of all types, ages, colours or race. But on this day the two strangers unnerved her. She raised her head from her writing to be aware suddenly of an incredible-looking 'car' outside the window. It had arrived in complete silence. She had heard no engine noise, no familiar crunching of the gravel on the approach drive or in the car park and no slamming of doors.

Her description of the 'car' tallied with that given by Caroline and Clinton. She could not place the make or origin of the vehicle, neither could she explain how it had come so silently, for even the arrival of a bicycle makes a noise on the loose gravel in the car park. Both strangers came to her reception desk and inquired whether Mrs Granville was in. She informed the strangers that she expected her mother back shortly if they would care to wait, but they expressed some urgency in keeping some other appointment and said that they could not stay very long; however, they would return.

Francine was struck by the remarkable similarity of the individuals when they stood side by side. They were the same height, with the same facial appearance, dress and hair style. She noticed particularly their smooth and white, almost transparent complexions, most unnatural in men, more like that of a woman with a very fine skin. There was no sign of beards or of shaving. She was also aware of their very penetrating, intelligent eyes. She found them to be serious and polite, quiet-spoken and unobtrusive. They had particularly fine hands, with long artistic-looking fingers and neatly trimmed nails which seemed to indicate that they had never undertaken physical labour. They departed in the same strange silent manner, the car leaving extremely quickly and without a sound.

Back at Ripperston Farm, Billy commented:

'I didn't believe in these things before, but I'll certainly believe in future. My wife wants to leave here now because she's frightened to death. It's the *closeness* of that sort of experience that's so frightening.'

Pauline reasoned:

'In a weird sort of way, we were almost getting used to the strange things that were happening. We'd all seen the same thing, analysed it, and come to the conclusion that if these people – creatures, or whatever they are – were going to harm us, they would have done so much earlier; and if they hadn't, maybe we had nothing to fear.'

Other strange intruders had been seen undertaking some kind of survey on the public highway. This had occurred on

176

the A48 two miles out of Carmarthen, towards Cross Hands.

At 2.30 on the morning of 27 August 1977, Francis Lloyd of Haverfordwest with his mate John Dwyer were driving their juggernaut east along the main road when they suddenly picked up in their headlights two of the 'giants' standing by the side of the road. Mr Lloyd pulled the lorry out a little and accelerated past the figures, unnerved by their appearance. Both were wearing onepiece suits made in some kind of translucent, bright red material and were extraordinary in size – he estimated at least 7 ft tall. Their features were not clear behind the usual visor. Mounted on one shoulder was a short stubby aerial about 12 inches long. Mr Lloyd and his co-driver, who are experienced travellers, had never encountered anything like this before. In addition they spoke of a marked drop in temperature as they passed the two figures. The truck sped on towards London, the two drivers silent. Mr Lloyd said that John Dwyer was quite upset by the experience and did not wish to talk about it afterwards.

A consistent factor which I noted throughout the descriptions of these encounters was that there were always two figures, never more, never less: two figures on the road out of Carmarthen; two visitors who tried to contact the witnesses; two figures emerging from the UFO late at night outside the Haven Fort Hotel; two figures on Stack Rocks. The obvious conclusion was that the installation at Stack Rocks and the majority of the UFOs that were being observed were controlled by two individuals; in the 'Welsh Triangle' possibly the same two on each occasion. It was of course the logical number of persons to have, as for example when the Americans sent two astronauts to the moon, one to assist the other in case of difficulty.

Where numerous UFOs had been seen, and in the case of Pauline Coombs's encounter with the 'flying football', the small dimensions of the craft obviously indicated some form of automatic aerial mechanism. But the most intriguing feature of all was the description by Caroline Class, Clinton

Coombs, and Francine Granville, three completely disconnected witnesses and none of them interested in the UFOs, that the two visitors had been identical.

The chances of their being twins seemed remote and I recalled other incidents where the visitors had borne exact similarity of features. Without going into details of those in the USA that I recall I shall mention briefly a case which I myself investigated extensively and which took place in the West Country. The witness was a Mr Bryant of Scoriton. I should state that some inconsistencies have been noted in the Bryant story since his death. He died a few years after his encounter, which occurred on 24 May 1965. However, I find that the minor variations in his account are shown only on circumstantial evidence; and on the basis of my own investigations I consider that the man, although not highly educated and possibly embellishing his story here and there, was, in the main, telling the truth. So many pieces of Bryant's story were confirmed afterwards that I am inclined to believe it. Another contributory factor in my giving credence to his story is that I independently located another witness who saw the space vehicle depart and overfly his farm at Dartington some eleven miles distant from the Bryant encounter. The descriptions of the two craft tallied exactly.

Bryant was out walking in deserted moorland about one mile from his house when he was confronted by the appearance of a huge dome-shaped craft with a curved underside, hovering at about 30 ft over a nearby field. Initially he thought it to be a Russian spacecraft, as at the time the Russians were making considerable propaganda out of their space flights; so when the craft descended and hovered at a height of 3 ft above the field Bryant did not instinctively run but looked on with inquisitive gaze. A door slid upwards and three figures appeared, all wearing spacesuits. They beckoned to him. Bryant approached the craft, which he estimated to be 50 ft in diameter, and was addressed by the smallest and youngest-looking of the three occupants, who had now removed their helmets and were breathing with some slight difficulty. The accent of the individuals was not determinable by Bryant but it certainly seemed to cause some problems with communication and many of the words and sentences that he related back to me did not make any sense to him at the time, as the terms were not in common use.

However, Bryant was assisted aboard the craft and remained there for approximately forty-five minutes, while his host tried to explain a number of issues to him. It is a great pity that Bryant's limited education and experience did not allow him fully to comprehend what was being told him or even to take any real part in the conversation. He was able only to listen and relate afterwards, haltingly and in a disarrayed jigsaw of disconnected ideas and words, the information which had been so painstakingly communicated. It took many hours of discussion and re-enactment of the events to extract anything near the original information and when it did emerge the facts seemed too incredible to be true.

Of the three individuals one differed considerably in appearance. He was the smallest, resembling a teenager, with dark hair and of normal human appearance. It was this ufonaut who did all the talking and apparently was the only member of the crew who spoke English. The other two, who were considerably taller, had long high craniums and blond hair down to their shoulders. Although apparently masculine they were slightly feminine-looking, with fair complexions. They had very unusual eyes, which Bryant thought may have had a vertical cat-like iris as opposed to the human circular pupil. Both these ufonauts were as similar as identical twins.

The translator claimed that the craft was operated from a facility sited on the planet Venus, although he made no indication that this was the home of the ufonauts or where the vessel had been constructed. Bryant inquired as to the motive power but was given only a vague description: some method of control was employed which allowed the pilot to operate the craft directly by thought waves as distinct from manual control. This apparently was quicker and more reliable, although manual methods could provide a secondary back-up system.

In this day and age of infrared switches and artificial limbs operated by brain waves, none of this information came as a particular surprise, but was seen more as a logical progression of servo-control.

The translator communicated a certain amount of information on their culture, and the education and policies of the controlling power which operated the vessel, but most of this apparently was beyond Bryant's comprehension. One could only summarize that the general feeling was a benevolent one towards the human race, with concern over our cultural evolution and dangers which they, as external observers, could see in better perspective than ourselves.

Despite translation difficulties the communicator tried to relay to Bryant some information regarding another source of interstellar vessels which were using the airspace in the vicinity of the planet Earth. He claimed that these other craft originated from the star Epsilon Eridani, a star just over ten light-years from our sun. The translator stated that the individuals coming to Earth from this star could jump long distances and were capable of becoming invisible.

Science fiction stuff supposedly, but when one looks at the evidence of the real events, it seems remarkably like the truth. The strange visitors to Ripperston Farm in the 'Welsh Triangle' indeed did seem to be able to cover long distances very quickly although it does not seem likely that they physically jumped; rather, that they used some mechanical aid or even teleportation. Similarly the departure of the 'car' was extremely curious and the teleportation events concerning the cows again suggest that the process of becoming invisible or eluding observation is available to the ufonauts. So when the translator innocently said that they could jump long distances and become invisible maybe he was grappling with the English language. He also made a curious statement that the purpose of the visitors was for 'procreation' and this has always left researchers in some doubt as to its exact meaning. The strange thing is that many of the incidents I have investigated subsequent to the Bryant encounter in 1965 have borne out the information which he in fact related. This we will analyse in greater detail in the final chapter.

However, to return to the Bryant encounter specifically: the witness noticed that the craft was divided into sections in which some form of television screen was present and this his host indicated was a method of monitoring the control of the craft. Noticeable in the vessel too, as is also recounted of nearly all other craft of this type, was a central axial pillar, apparently an integral part of the drive-mechanism.

When Bryant had departed from the UFO he returned home in a subdued and perplexed frame of mind. The incident certainly had done him no good physically, in the sense that after that his life was one perpetual problem. The story which he at first kept to himself eventually leaked out via a chance comment which brought police, newsmen and UFO investigators knocking on his door for two years before ill-health eventually took him from this world.

Little was gained from the Bryant experience by the field of ufological research at the time. Controversy and disagreement raged between individual investigators and other than the initial sensational few lines in the local press, the story was forgotten by the general public after a few weeks. A subsequent book written about the affair did little to add to the clarity of the situation. I knew that Bryant did not trust UFO investigators and I felt that after the initial leaking of the story he had in fact made personal attempts to duck out from the public limelight by causing diversions of his own manufacture. Bryant was not a publicity seeker, he never made a single penny out of his experiences, and his life became a misery after them. I have the greatest sympathy for the man and throughout the remaining years of his life I valued him as a distant but genuine acquaintance. Allegedly the UFO returned to Bryant and dropped to him some aircraft parts which proved as enigmatic as the original 'messages'. The pieces unfortunately fell quickly into the hands of others and were subsequently lost or destroyed by amateurish experimentation. One line of inquiry which was pursued at the time was that they were part of an aircraft which had been fragmented by a UFO accident in the early 1950s. Considerable lengths were gone to, to prove this point and I was convinced all along that it was a complete red herring. I feel that the significance of the mechanisms that were dropped to Bryant were as a clue and a puzzle, a piece in a jigsaw to which one would have to apply one's intelligence and intuition in order to derive the answer. Bryant was one of the other 'small people in a very big game'. He was threatened by a thickset man with an American accent, perhaps a member of the CIA, to forget his story or else, and was eventually discredited, as is the general policy with UFO witnesses. But the information which he had conveyed, however small and fragmented, subsequently was verified by other events.

Duncan Lunan in his speculations regarding the radio communications which were picked up in 1927* has suggested that the probe which he considered was circling the earth had identified itself as coming from the star Epsilon Boötes and it was pointed out by one astronomer that looking from that area of the sky towards our own sun we ourselves might be included within the Epsilon constellation. The general implication is that we are dealing with interstellar travellers who live relatively in our own backyard, no more than ten or twelve light-years away, and within our immediate star group. Lunan further suggested that the endeavours of the travellers were not purely intellectual exploration but might be motivated by the fundamental drive to survive if their own home conditions had started to prove difficult. I do not personally think this is true but I feel there is the definite possibility that one source of these space

* Detailed in *Man and the Stars* by Duncan Lunan. Published in paperback by Corgi in 1978.

travellers is interested in producing a marriage of the two
civilizations which so far has been blocked by the great
disparity between their culture and ours.

Were Bryant's communicators representatives of some
kind of interstellar United Nations which was concerned
with allowing the human race to evolve to a higher point
naturally, without too much foreign interference?

I am convinced that the source of the UFO cannot be
narrowed down to a single point but constitutes at least two
different and divergent origins having a very real interest in
the continuation of the biosphere of this green and fertile
planet. For this reason I am certain that 'they' are keeping a
very careful eye on mankind's management or mismanage-
ment of its resources and technology. The degree to which
'they' already influence our lives every day, hopefully for our
protection and good, I shall discuss in another book,* but
for the moment let us concentrate on the events in the 'Welsh
Triangle'.

12

Daughters of Heaven

During the course of our pre-production programme for
Professor Hans Holzer's film *The Ufonauts*, Jane and I
travelled to Birmingham to meet a man with a most curious
and enlightening story. He enjoyed the rather grand name of
Commander Horatio Penrose, RN Rtd, and the event which
he detailed to us, although it had taken place a few years
previously, was one of the most informative accounts that
we had received so far. He was pleasant, unassuming, intelligent and interested in the nature of our researches.

* *UFO-UK*. New English Library.

Subsequent to his experience he had become interested in UFOs and throughout his life he had taken an active interest in the study of hypnosis.

The story he had to tell us concerned an encounter which had taken place shortly before midnight on Thursday, 13 May 1954. He had been driving his 1953 black Vauxhall Wyvern saloon back towards his home, which was at that time more towards Derby, along the main Derby–Burton road in the direction of Birmingham. The time was approximately 10.30 p.m. and he was approaching the Hilton Gravel works near Burmaston. He was alarmed to see approaching him at high speed and apparently head on to the line of his vehicle, a very bright light above the level of the road. He thought it could be a car, but its position puzzled him. He slowed, but before he could take any effective action, the object had halted above his vehicle and caused his car to stop so abruptly that he was thrown forward in the driving seat and hit his head against the windscreen. He was conscious that his vehicle had left the highway. It seemed to be held in midair, by an object that was gripping it somehow magnetically by virtue of the metal roof, which naturally, considering the weight of the vehicle, was distorting and bending the body of the car. Although dazed, he was aware that the vehicle was moving slightly. It was then lowered to the side of the road. It seems that for all intents and purposes the Commander was describing the first recorded traffic 'accident' between a UFO and a ground vehicle, after which the UFO seems to have picked up the vehicle and moved it out of the way of any other traffic which might come along.

The Commander was then aware of a man in a onepiece suit lifting him effortlessly from the car, and carrying him somehow upward through an entrance in the underside of a large circular craft – the same UFO which had caused the 'accident' and which was hovering directly overhead. Commander Penrose particularly remembers the bright light which was coming from the entrance and enabling him to see the surroundings of the 'crash'. The curious moving of the vehicle off the road had in fact been independently witnessed by a British Railways signalman from the first-floor level of his signal box some short distance down the road. He remembers having seen a car with an 'extremely bright light above it' go past his signal box at about the same level. Rather too high off the ground for an ordinary kind of accident!

The Commander found himself being taken into a brightly lit room and laid on a table for medical attention. Situated around the walls of the room were various control mechanisms and the craft was being operated by about five people, both male and female, who did not appear unusual to him except that they were of slightly shorter stature than the average British citizen, being more of the height common to the Japanese race; likewise, they had slightly almond-shaped eyes. All the operators were wearing similar 'catsuits', he thought blue in colour, and their dark hair was conventionally short and straight.

He was attended to by one of the female operators, an attractive and shapely girl who appeared to be in her late twenties and who was sympathetic towards his injuries. The Commander had received a nasty cut on his forehead, minor cuts and bruises and slight concussion as a result of hitting the car windscreen.

The witness was particularly struck by the girl operator's flawless white skin and even more amazed by her brilliant ability to communicate with him telepathically. How this was achieved he had no idea, but he was very strongly aware of her thoughts and she seemed capable of reading his mind instantly as he thought of questions to ask her. During his treatment, which included an injection of some green fluid into his arm, he queried her as to the propulsion system of the curious craft. He received some answer involving the use of gyroscopic mechanisms employing magnetic fields. The woman asked him questions about his position and the Commander answered cautiously, wondering whether his strange benefactors could be from some foreign power, as the woman seemed interested in his work in the Navy with radar and questioned him closely on this point. The Commander, evading the issue somewhat, countered with more precise questions about the nature of the vehicle but seemed unable to appreciate the detail which was given, or possibly the woman similarly evaded his inquiries.

There was not much time for 'conversation' but one of the items which came up was a curious statement by the woman that they were not born in the same manner as we are. The Commander was more interested in obtaining useful information about the vessel's engineering and tried some of his knowledge of hypnosis to penetrate the woman's mind, but apparently this was not well received and he remembers shortly afterwards passing out, seemingly under the effects of some sedative drug which had been administered. Although he remained unconscious for only a very short time, he remembers being returned to his vehicle in a very groggy condition. The car was then moved again and supposedly lowered or even dropped a short distance onto some upright iron railings.

The details of the entire episode and 'crash' are somewhat vague. Exactly where the vehicle left the road originally or came to rest while the Commander was taken up for medical attention and then subsequently dropped seems a little unclear. However, a press picture taken of the vehicle afterwards shows the rear end of the Vauxhall resting on and perched above the upright iron railings adjoining the road with the majority of the vehicle on the opposite side to the highway. The Vauxhall shows considerable distortion to the roof as if some giant magnet had pulled it upwards. The bonnet hood is also shown pulled upwards and there is considerable damage to the nearside door, nearside front wing and the lefthand side of the vehicle. There also seems to be some evidence of a lamp-post having been demolished, presumably when the vehicle was either being bounced around by the impact of the UFO's 'field' or when it was being carried along deliberately or accidentally underneath the alien craft. It does seem clear, however, that the dropping of the car from the UFO after the encounter was from a height which certainly did not do the vehicle or its occupant much good.

The *Derby Evening Telegraph* which carried a report of the incident at the time, if only in its simple and uncontroversial form, said: 'There was no one at Hilton Gravel works when the accident occurred, and the gates – specially widened for heavy lorries – stood open. If the car had left the road a few seconds earlier it would have gone through the open gates without encountering any obstacle.'

Apparently the Commander had been found by an RAC driver. Police at the time were interested in an inexplicable point: inside the Vauxhall was found an extraordinary amount of blood, far more than could have come from the Commander's body without his having died from the loss of it. Police were concerned that maybe a second person may have been in the vehicle and had walked away dazed by the crash and in need of attention. But there had been no passenger. Commander Penrose had been travelling alone. The presence of the blood remained a mystery. It was almost as though the witness had received a massive transfusion during the course of his medical treatment, allowing him to lose the quantity of plasma found without a surely fatal result.

At the time the Commander kept the more unacceptable aspects of the story to himself, as he feared that he might be ridiculed and lose his job. However, at no time has he sought publicity or any reward for his claims and it is only now after many years have passed and the atmosphere and feeling towards such reports has become more tolerant that he has allowed the story to be made known.

One wonders how many other similar events lie waiting to be revealed by members of the general public?

In agriculture these days artificial insemination and other technical methods are commonly employed and if it is in fact possible to reproduce children other than by the normal methods of birth, which we enjoy along with all the other mammals, then it does not seem unreasonable that an advanced civilization may have developed and taken advantage of them. Commander Penrose suffered some memory loss after his encounter and even now cannot recall all the details surrounding the event, but he remembers some slight reference by his alien 'nurse' to subtle differences in the ufonauts' bodies compared with our own.

Another incident, which occurred on 6 January 1976, apparently involved the deliberate inducement of memory loss after the event. Louise Smith, Mona Stafford and Elaine Thomas were returning from a quiet dinner celebration at 11.30 p.m. along highway 78 out of Stanford, Kentucky when they experienced an encounter with a UFO which involved them in an unaccountable loss of time of over an hour. Exactly what happened during that period is not fully known, but hypnotic regression which has been undertaken on the women, all in their mid thirties, indicates that some kind of medical examination was carried out by the ufonauts. The witnesses suffered sunburn, skin and eye irritation after the event. A curious factor which may give a clue as to the nature of the operation carried out on them is that one of the women had ended her menstrual period six days before the event, but on the day following the encounter menstrual bleeding began again and she had the usual abdominal cramps. What could have triggered this we shall discuss after the introduction of the following and most specific case.

This information came to me by way of a most confidential approach from a young woman. Following an article that I had written for a local newspaper, Mrs X, as I shall be obliged to call her, telephoned me and requested an appointment to see me as she sought my assistance over a problem which had troubled her for many years. She would give me no more details at that time and it was not until several weeks later that I met her in her home and the full implications of the story became apparent. One condition of her trust was that I would never reveal her name or expose her to publicity without her prior agreement. And this I have rigorously adhered to, for up to this point in time, other than my original investigation, only one other researcher and an eminent parapsychologist have had any knowledge of the case.

I found Mrs X to be a country girl, married, with three children. She was tall, good-looking, dark-haired, intelligent and shy. She knew that she had experienced a unique encounter which she could not fully understand; neither could she relate it to any of her relatives, friends, or even her doctor without being openly ridiculed or considered insane. However, the suppression of the experience within her was causing considerable psychological stress, and she felt that she had to tell somebody, to discuss the relevance of what had happened and seek reassurance that no harm might have ensued.

One of her problems was that after the initial incident she had only partial memory of what had happened and only snatches of the incident had come to her over the years, breaking through a strong subconscious wall in her to suppress the experience. Her husband was a little incredulous of its reality but he had not been a witness specifically and therefore was not in a position to help. At the first meeting we discussed the subject only in very general terms and made an appointment for a few weeks later when, with her husband present, I could partially hypnotically regress her and autosuggest that this mental block be gently released and the incident examined, to reveal conscious knowledge of what had transpired. This regression was remarkably successful, as I found that such was the pressure in Mrs X's subconscious to unburden herself of the feelings of anxiety resulting from the event, that she was an easy subject and responded quickly. Subsequent to this I also arranged for her to relate the incident consciously on tape – that is, the information she had now managed to recall to the front of her mind and having achieved this I then decided that it was best to leave the memory as it stood and not harass her further as this would cause a relapse in her psychological health. I can state emphatically that Mrs X is 100 per cent sane and sincere and is not suffering from any kind of delusions or fantasies.

My word of honour to Mrs X forbids me to reveal where this incident took place, although she has now moved from that particular village; or when exactly it occurred. The full story, put together from all the hypnotic regressions and interviews, is as follows:

Mrs X is a very happily married woman. She had borne her husband two children whilst living a rural life in a quiet and remote country village 200 to 300 miles west of London. Her first child had been born when she was quite young and when this incident occurred she was still a woman in her twenties. She was pregnant with her third child (which subsequently was born a beautiful little girl), when the first incident took place:

'I think it was a fortnight before my baby was born. I was taking my two children for a walk and I had this terrible – I suppose I was a bit giddy – very funny feeling, and I looked up and above the tree I could see this silvery thing, and I thought it was an aeroplane. I find it difficult . . . I just can't . . . I thought it was an aeroplane and . . . but realized there was no noise with it, and with that, it sort of went away, and I was petrified then, and I took the girls on up the hill and I was so scared I came back home.'

The first experience by Mrs X seems to have been a conventional UFO encounter of the first kind. Mrs X recalls very little about the first encounter and other than her being scared I think that in terms of actual information there is little to be gained from this first event. Its significance to our story specifically is that she was visited by the alien craft two weeks before her child was born and this has a bearing on the later story.

After the birth of her third child she has not conceived

any other children, out of anxiety that some complication might arise out of a new pregnancy, as a result of her experiences.

The second and vital encounter occurred one evening after the birth when she had been discharged from hospital and was now at home.

She recounts: 'I had a terrible feeling – it was after the baby was born. About twelve days after Penelope was born I had a feeling that something was going to happen that evening, a terrible strong feeling that something was going to happen ... I just can't think straight ... I went out into the kitchen and washed the nappies and went to hang them out ... into the garden to hang up some nappies and I think I'd hung up the second one when ... I was on the second one and had a feeling that someone was watching me and I turned around and in the sky was this orange-red ball. Well, like a very bright star. So, I turned around and started to peg up the other nappies and still had this terrible feeling to turn around and have a look. And with that, it started to move and went around the sky, and with that at a terrific speed it started coming towards me.

'And I thought, My God, it's a helicopter or something and it's going to crash. And I was really petrified then, and I thought, My end's come, I'm going to die, you know. And with that it stopped dead. But I think I was in such a panic, so scared I thought, Well, is this dying, am I dying now? Because I was so scared, and with that it started hovering.

'I think it went to the left of me and all these bright-coloured lights started coming from it. Blue and pink, well, it was really lovely to look at and then there was this white silvery bubble or something, really beautiful, thrown over me and I seemed to be walking in it as well. But I can't remember ... I think it must have come around to the right of me and then I saw, I thought I saw, somebody staring at me – enormous eyes, just looking at me.'

In the course of another session she related the experience over to me again and from this I was able to deduce that the craft had appeared first of all as a red-coloured star, moving about at high speed, and then coming directly towards her, getting alarmingly larger and causing her the fear that it was an aircraft about to crash. When it came to the end of her garden, which overlooks open fields, it stopped and hovered at about 30 ft above the ground. At this time she could see through a large panoramic window the figure of a tall man, dressed in some dark uniform, looking down at her with his hands separated and pressed against the glass of the window. He was staring at her. It was at this point that she had become transfixed and experienced the almost hallucinogenic 'bubbles' which she described, and she felt that she was being hypnotized by the influence of the strange visitor. She described him as fairly good-looking, quite tall and slim, with black hair. She thought he was wearing a black silk cravat.

She continued: 'And trying . . . and as I was looking into these eyes I felt really good, you know. Then it comes to the left of me again and then, I suppose, I passed out or something.

'Then I can remember being picked up and I kept losing my shoe, and I was trying to tell them I was losing my right shoe but nobody would listen. I didn't lose the shoe and I suppose then I must have been up in this . . . up into this . . . thing! But I can't really tell you because you see all this had come to me after so many years. I couldn't remember these things right away.'

Mrs X described that she vaguely remembers after having 'passed out for a moment' how two of the ufonauts picked her up, one each side of her, and assisted her from the garden down into the field and up what she thinks must have been some kind of rope ladder into the craft. Her memory on this point is somewhat unclear. She remembers that the visitors were shorter than her (she is 5 ft 10 in) and they were 'definitely dressed' in onepiece suits, the colour of which she thought was a bluish grey. There seems to have been a loss of time at this point. The next she remembers is as she described:

'But up in this thing I seemed to be sitting on a table. The saucer itself was just ... it had windows in it, saucer-shaped, and windows along the front part; that's all I could really see, with the light shining out. Inside I sat on the end of a table and I can remember feeling cold, freezing cold and these chaps were all behind me. There must have been four or five of them. They were laughing; I felt ... laughing at me. Then they started to pull at my hair and quite honestly, I thought they were Americans and well, Americans really, and yet I don't know how they were talking.'

The majority of the crew seemed to be amused by the situation and joked freely amongst themselves and with her although she could not understand their language and it was upon this point that she could not justify to herself that they were indeed 'Americans'. The individual who had initially hypnotized her calmed the other members of the crew down, seeming to be concerned that she was becoming hysterical at this hilarity at her expense. The time of year was summer and there was no reason for her to have felt obviously 'cold' unless for one simple reason which will become obvious. This is another point which has been blocked in her sub-conscious and is as unacceptable now as it was then.

She continued: 'And then there was somebody, this terrible ugly chap came out, and then I really got hysterical. But all this time I was never really awake; I was in a semi-daze all the time.'

As well as the four or five normal-looking 'human beings' there now appeared a man who obviously was not of ter-restrial or human origin. So strange was this to her that up to this time all attempts at extracting details from her subconscious memory have failed.

She went on: 'But it was my fingers, my hand; they did something with my right hand. I don't know whether they cut it. I don't know, because it was the following day that I

193

remembered I had a cut on my finger and I didn't know how I had done it.'

Mrs X recalls that there were a number of surgical instruments near to her and it seems highly likely by her direct memories and recollections of the following day that a blood sample was taken from one of the fingers of her right hand. It is possible with regard to the 'hair pulling' incident that a sample of hair may have been taken also.

She went on: 'Whatever else was it, they laid me back and they were going to do something to me, but I said it would hurt, and they said "No . . ." I don't know. I must have gone out then.'

Another session with Mrs X brought more details of this significant point in the operation. She described to me in detail a laproscope, a long tube-like device equipped with optical facilities for allowing a surgeon to insert the tube inside the body and view the interior through an eyepiece attached to the instrument. The significant thing is that this detailed description was given several years before the instrument was in fact developed and came into use in our present-day medical technology. There was no way at the time of her dictation that Mrs X could have known or could have anticipated the use of such an instrument. She recalls that the laproscope was to be inserted through her navel for an internal examination, when she passed out or was sedated further. Subsequent examination confirmed that she had bled slightly from a small incision in the navel and the implication and likelihood is that this method of entry was used to find an area in her abdomen in proximity to her ovaries. It seems likely with regard to the other information available and the subsequent series of events, that the purpose of the operation was to remove at least one egg from her, bearing in mind that it was a fortnight after the birth of her baby and that she would be in a fertile condition.

It was not until July 1978 that Dr Steptoe in Oldham, Lancashire was successful in producing the first test-tube baby by removing eggs from the mother and fertilizing them externally in the laboratory prior to inserting them in the womb of a recipient, who then proceeded to have a normal pregnancy. The purpose of this modern research technique is to bypass blockages in the Fallopian tubes which normally produce infertility in a woman by restricting the passage of the eggs down to the womb.

In the case of Mrs X her fertility had of course been proved and the purpose of the operation (which was by a technology very similar to if not in advance of that used by Dr Steptoe) seems to have been to remove eggs from her ovaries for external fertilization and either to transplant them or to use them for some other method of embryo cultivation. The comment made by the 'nurse' in the case of Commander Penrose, regarding the fact that the UFO operators were not born in the 'normal' way, now becomes highly significant when considered in relation to this later piece of information.

Mrs X continued: 'When I came round they asked me if I knew two foreign names. One was a George and another foreign name, and I said, "No! No, I've never heard of them." '

She went on: 'But I can picture now what the inside of the "saucer" was like. There was this table thing in the middle of the room and I think behind me were the controls, and there must have been a small door out into the control room or where the windows were. And there was something when I came in at the door. There was something on the right of me where they were all standing. And this ugly chap, this terrible-looking person, was standing. I can't really remember anything else about that, just that I was freezing cold, freezing. It was very cold in there.'

Mrs X related more easily now: 'Well I seemed to be walking down the path with one on each . . . a man each side of me . . . and they took me to the door; and just . . . well . . . they said something. Oh! No! . . . when I was in the spacecraft, when I was just going in at the door, they said, "We want to see if you have had your baby." Well, I can't remember the exact words, but I said, "I've had my baby!" But I don't know who I was talking to. Because ... I just don't know who I was talking to. But I said, "I've had my baby!" And I think that's what they were doing when I passed out, or they did something to put me out. They might have been examining me, or something, but when I was coming down from the spacecraft these two chaps were either side of me and they took me to the back door. And I was feeling fine. And they said something about, "That wasn't so bad was it?" '

As Mrs X continued to surface the memories which she had so long suppressed, facts would emerge and flashes of memory occur after pieces of the story had gone by, rather like pieces of driftwood floating up from the muddy bed of a river.

She continued: 'And I was very happy and just as I was going to go inside the door they hit me on the back of the neck and with the force I sort of dropped inside the door, but I picked myself up quick and ran up the step and said to Peter, "Come out here! I've just seen something. You must come quick!" And well, he didn't come quick enough. No. We'll have to get this right. Before I shouted to him, I think I looked out around the door again and there was something going off, but it was all so quick.

'But I saw some smoke. The spacecraft went and I saw this smoketrail behind, but by the time Peter got out, that had vanished as well. But that's all I can tell you about that. But when I came in I said to him, "I've seen a thing and I am sure it's a UFO, a spacecraft." '

When Mrs X was asked the question: 'Could you describe the people in the spacecraft a little more?' she answered: 'I find it difficult to think. The peculiar thing about it is, that when I got into the kitchen, I wanted to tell him everything ... and everything seemed to be blocked. I just couldn't tell him anything, but I did go down to the toilet and started to examine myself. But I thought, they couldn't have seen me. No, of course, they didn't look at me. But I had a strong feeling, just little bits coming back, but I couldn't remember the full story to tell anybody. But things kept cropping up ... but they couldn't have looked at me. No! No, nothing happened. You know, I kept trying then to convince myself that nothing had happened. But the following day I woke up in the morning and Oh! terrible runs, you know, diarrhoea. Fright? I don't know. Because this went on for three days; but that next day I think we were all very sick, and well, I think Peter was the first one to be sick.'

Despite the suppression in her mind of what had actually happened, Mrs X could not subdue the feeling that some kind of internal examination had been carried out. It was while she was examining herself that she noticed a slight trickle of blood from her navel, as if a local anaesthetic had been administered, although she felt no pain. The diarrhoea trouble could have been just fright but the fact that her husband and family also contracted it suggests a cross infection from some bacteria which, apparently, lasted for three days. Subsequent to her experience Mrs X suffered some thinning and loss of hair and a deterioration in the condition of her fingernails, suggestive of radiation effects but equally possibly due to psychological factors resulting from a heavily implanted post-hypnotic suggestion that she should forget the experience. Due also to the anxiety factor, she lost weight and had some difficulty in sleeping. Further, after the encounter, she underwent a complete nine-month false pregnancy during which she neither menstruated nor gave any indication superficially that she was not in fact pregnant. Together with this she experienced mounting anxiety as she approached the 'phantom' birth and a sense of relief and an intuitive kinship with her unknown child afterwards. Even now Mrs X has the definite feeling that she has four children, not just her own three.

But to finish her story:

'Oh! I've forgotten to tell you something. They told me to take my clothes off and put them in a wardrobe, and my shoes ... but I mean, I didn't have that many clothes, I had to wear these things again. It was the following day. Things kept cropping up; you see, I've told the story, what I can remember, now, but at the time I couldn't remember these things. I can't really tell you what the people looked like. I just thought that the men who brought me down from the spacecraft were very much like ourselves, perhaps not quite as tall as I was. But perhaps I should try and remember the day after.

'Oh! The name George kept coming up. George. I don't know any Georges. Well there's a boy called George, but I didn't know . . . Well, I knew it was a foreign name but I just couldn't remember the name.'

'What I think, well, I think; I was becoming ill really because I was suppressing something, you know, and I think it was the dreams, the psychic dreams . . . the terrible psychic dreams. One was about this man and another was that my daughter was going to be carried high.'

The reference to 'George' and the foreign surname implies that the ufonauts were familiar with our own UFO literature or it may infer more about a certain well-known man. The controversy that surrounded the most famous 'contact', George Adamski, rages to this day and the more I hear, the more problems arise. Through his lifelong associate Desmond Leslie we learn that Adamski had poor eyesight; and when reading the literature produced by Adamski one can see that possibly if it were Adamski himself who was making many of the assumptions, coupled with his difficulty with vision, many of his alleged errors could be explained. I still tend to think that many of the uncannily accurate facts which Adamski brought out in his writings, such as that of the 'fireflies', which were only subsequently verified and confirmed by the US astronauts while orbiting the Earth, do suggest that there is more in Adamski's writings than pure fantasy.

The reference by Mrs X to her dreams is another clear indication of her locked-up memories surfacing through her subconscious mind in a dream state, suppressed and confined to that region by the hypnotic suggestions that she had absorbed.

She finished her recollections: 'And this was all going to happen in twelve years. And, of course, she was a carnival queen – they call it the May Queen – and she was carried high. And she was a special child.

'I think, really, I became ill with keeping it in. In fact, when we moved house I did go to the doctor and he just laughed at me as if to say, "We've got a right one here." In fact you're the first person I've told and I feel a lot better for telling you. But there must be other things I can tell you. I should have written it down.' She finished, still struggling to recall the other information locked up deep in the recesses of her mind.

Mrs X's transcript clearly shows two factors at work. One is her suppressed recollections surfacing in limited flashes to which she then almost immediately adds a logical explanation. For example, she clearly recalls a prediction about her daughter being 'carried high', and immediately justifies this by referring to her third child, who some years later was chosen as the May Queen and was carried above the heads of the townspeople on the carnival float. But the latter is purely an explanation for a flash of recollection which she cannot immediately explain. In my opinion it refers to her 'fourth daughter', if indeed it was another girl, and of her being carried high to some unknown place in the stars.

Her third daughter, the child who had been born just before the encounter, has grown up into a perfectly normal and healthy ebullient youngster, while her 'fourth child' has never returned. Mrs X was subsequently visited some years later by another UFO which surveyed the house but did not make contact. Hopefully, her other-worldly child would by now be in her teens.

From the research work undertaken by Dr Steptoe and others into 'test-tube babies' we know that it is necessary for the egg taken from the ovary to develop in blood serum derived from the original mother, and this may well explain in Mrs X's case, and in others of which I have knowledge, why blood is taken when specimens of either eggs, or in the male case, sperm are donated.

Why the alien intelligences would wish to produce specimens of the human race, or a cross between the human race and their own, opens up a whole panorama of speculation. The individuals in the spacecraft which took aboard Mrs X were all between approximately twenty and thirty years of age, judging from appearance, and were, supposedly, in excellent health. The slight suggestion of radioactivity, if indeed that was the case, would of course produce sterility in both male and female occupants exposed for long periods of time and one could be dealing with a situation where a race travelling space had become burdened with the problem of sterility after years of working in a radiation-exposed environment. Therefore, are the experiments in this connection towards the furtherance of their own race or indeed is the human race so nearly related to our alien cousins that interrelationships are a simple matter? Some writers have suggested that mankind on this planet originated from a point external from our solar system and was introduced here many thousands of years ago by interstellar colonists. Other writers have suggested that humans are indeed a cross breed of some race indigenous to Earth, a kind of man-ape, that was in some way assisted on its evolutionary path either by a direct DNA genetic intervention or by simple injection of extra-terrestrial bloodstock. Such legends as the 'sons of God coming down to marry the daughters of men' may suggest this kind of origin. But the question still arises as to why in this twentieth century should the exercise need to be revised and repeated.

Are the aliens undertaking a kind of anthropological rescue operation and insuring that specimens of the human race are preserved and kept alive in some external colony just in case we are successful in blowing ourselves to bits – a project on which unfortunately so many national governments seem determined to waste a large percentage of their gross national product? Or is it simply that the alien intelligences themselves are too far removed from our evolution in their normal bodies and need to produce an inter-racial stock of people to allow them to communicate adequately and on a permanent basis in the future?

On the other hand there are writers who would claim that this is all an intrigue leading towards an eventual invasion of the planet Earth. I discount this idea on the simple basis of the obvious patience of the alien interlopers. One can find examples of alien and human cross-breeding not only in the Bible but also in other early works, and in medieval times, even in myths and legends of European and oriental magic. I would suggest that the aliens have no incentive or even advantage in colonizing the planet Earth, as indeed their technology seems to place them considerably beyond the practical problems which face us here from day to day. However, they may well face serious problems of their own and in this connection the human race may have much to give them; similarly, they could contribute to us in terms of their own culture.

Flexibility and insight into the variety of backgrounds which could give rise to a very advanced civilization must be sustained in order not to reject these inter-relationships out of hand. One can view these 'experiments' emotionally, intellectually, even morally. But either way they have taken place, and they have in the main produced very little ill effect on those involved, other than psychological ones, which were mostly placed on the witnesses by the society in which they live, a society which makes the relating of their experiences extremely difficult. I am personally convinced that mankind is an interstellar race, that in fact man here owes much of his origin, evolution and technological progress to influences from outside the planet Earth. I do not think that human beings are so brilliant as to evolve suddenly to this point of technological superiority within the last few decades without some external assistance. A brief examination of some of the spontaneous 'inspirations' ove the previous hundred years would lend weight, I am sure to this hypothesis.

Where then is it all leading, to what are we being educated and what is the success rate and the likelihood of a satis factory result? Is the planet Earth slowly being absorbed into a 'cosmic club' which has been sending surveyors and explorers to this planet for millennia and now deems tha we are sufficiently advanced to become fuller members o that supposedly vast organization? Or are we to remain ir the backwoods of the universe?

I think all these questions could be answered before the advent of the twenty-first century. Some of the answers wil neither be acceptable to the present-day pundits nor deemed desirable by government leaders who would prefer to re main very much in their own shell. But it is obvious, from the researches that I have carried out, that the alier intelligences singular or multiple are carrying out a vast programme not sporadically but every day of the week. Some aspects of it we have been examining here and some other aspects I shall examine in other works; but one thing is apparent purely from the number of incidents I have logged in this one short volume, and that is that the intensity of activity is far greater than the general public has ever realized and that to suppress this one startling fact various government departments have gone to considerable trouble.

In conclusion I would like to refer to another major account which has shed light on our researches. With respect to the witness I shall again withhold her address, and name. She was kind enough to write to me in response to another newspaper appeal. Her letter reads:

Dear Mr Paget,

Thank you for your letter dated 15 February and I'm glad to hear that you've had so many letters. I envy you your job of reading them.

Before I tell you my experiences I would just like to say

that I was a member of the Royal Observer Corps for three years in the 1960s. I had to be able to identify every aircraft in the world within 4 seconds of each other flashed on a screen and I did pretty well in these tests.

I live on a large council estate which is situated on fairly high ground. There is a very high pylon on the edge of the adjoining common. I believe it is called a telecommunications 'tower'. It is lit up at night with red lights and is a landmark for miles around. So this pylon could be attracting UFOs.

The common is used quite frequently for army exercises both day and night, so I'm used to the flares and the firing.

We also have air traffic flying over us daily from the nearby aerodrome.

On the evening of 20 August 1974, 9.45, my husband and I took our dog for a walk. We were passing a school on our estate when my husband pointed to something above the Youth Centre. It had many coloured stationary lights around it which flashed brightly one after the other. I can't remember the exact colour sequence now, but I do remember the colours themselves – they were blue, orange, green, red and white. The lights pulsated brightly from left to right and the object was oscillating slightly as if some part of it was rotating. I would say it was about one hundred feet up and as I was taking this all in it moved towards us as if it had spotted us watching, and as it moved the pulsating lights speeded up.

The object then took off in an easterly direction over the school playing fields. I immediately urged my husband to let me run to the phone box to call the police so they could look out for it, but my husband wouldn't let me.

While we were standing there arguing, the object changed direction and came back westerly, then south, then north towards us, then west again. Then we lost sight of it behind some trees – behind the Youth Centre.

We had watched it for a good ten minutes and even my

203

husband who is extremely sceptical about such things had to admit that it couldn't possibly be an aeroplane or a helicopter. The object made no noise at all and the air traffic that evening was passing over the common behind us from east to west and there was no mistaking them with all the noise they made. The object was pretty large, about 40 ft wide, but we couldn't see any shape against the starry sky, the lights were too bright; but going by the way the lights pulsated and quickened, I'd say it was disc-shaped.

There was a large bright moon that evening in the east and you could see nearly all of the stars, there were only a few very high wispy clouds. There were some clouds to the northwest still tinged with pink from the setting sun.

I would just like to add that I've learnt of another eye witness who saw an object over the Youth Centre the same evening. He drives an ice-cream van and I know that they do still go around the estate late at night in the summer evenings, so I shall try to contact him as I'd like to hear what he has to say.

The next evening, 21 August 1974, I was watching the news, the time was 9.45, the children were all in bed and my husband was out and I had the urge to go out in the garden.

When I was half way down the garden path a very bright white light caught my eye to the right of me – I turned to face it – and saw what seemed to be a beam of white light like the landing light on a plane and it was approaching me, coming down below roof level. I immediately ran to the side of the house as I thought it was a light aircraft about to crash into our garden and on peeping round the corner of the house I saw this big ball of white light about 10 ft across stop dead above the spot on which I had been standing. It then went straight down the garden at about 15 to 20 ft in the air. It was then I heard a very low humming noise and I could see small red lights dotted about underneath it, but I couldn't make out the shape of it because of the very bright light.

I ran down the garden path after it feeling very brave and leapt on to the garden seat to get a better view over the 6-foot fence, as it was passing over the garden joining on to ours at the bottom, and would you believe it there were four or five more bright lights bobbing about in view between the houses; and this bright light joined the others, then went out of view behind the houses.

I then went indoors to take stock of things. The first thing I thought was, What is it? It did not have any wings. Why did I suddenly get up and go outside just at that particular moment?

Was this a warning? Or were they trying to prove to me that they existed? What would have happened to me if I'd stayed glued to the spot!

A neighbour of mine told me last year that her son Mark was playing up the garden with his friends one evening in August 1974, when a bright light swooped down on them and they all ran home frightened, and she said Mark wouldn't go out to play for several weeks afterwards.

When the weather turns really cold we put our five children into one large bedroom as it's cheaper to heat one room.

On Sunday morning 9 January this year [some years later] my youngest daughter Carol, just turned four years old, told me she had seen a man in the bedroom. I jokingly asked her, 'What man?' She said, 'The shining white man.'

I asked her to tell me what he looked like and from what she told me I ascertained that he wore a shiny onepiece suit with a polo neck, a belt with a torchlight in the centre, he had a long face, a head like 'Kojak', pointed ears, large eyes and he had a shining ball in one hand.

She said she sat on her pillow and watched him, and was only a little bit frightened of his face, especially the eyes. He walked around the bedroom and looked at each of the sleeping children in turn. He sat on Carol's bed and picked up her teddy bear and looked at it. He touched her on the tummy with the shiny ball, and he talked to her but she didn't know what he was saying. She said he threw the shiny ball and it disappeared, she thinks it went out into the garden.

I asked her if he went out of the bedroom, out of the door, but no, she said he just disappeared. When he'd gone she cried and got into bed with Angela and covered her head up.

I asked Angela what she remembered. She told me Carol was standing by her bed crying so she put her into bed with her and Carol had asked to have her head covered up.

To me this didn't sound much like the usual 'bogey man' story; if it was a dream then it was a strange, vivid one.

Also she wanted to go out into the garden to look for the shiny ball, she said she thought it must be broken up into tiny pieces, because the man had thrown it at the window.

I don't know what you will make of it but I think I shall just keep an open mind, I'm only glad she seems to have forgotten all about it now.

Thank you, Mr Paget, for letting me write to you of my experiences. I hope I have been of some assistance to you and I can't help wondering if anyone else has had similar experiences to mine.

Yours sincerely,
Mrs M

Yes, Mrs M, other people have had similar experiences, and I think you are very privileged along with your extraordinary little girl. Can I leave you with a quotation from another extraordinary person, Albert Einstein:

'The most beautiful thing we can experience is the mysterious. It is the source of all true art and science.'

MYSTERIES OF THE UNIVERSE – REVEALED

Charles Berlitz

Without a Trace	95p ☐
The Mystery of Atlantis	85p ☐
The Bermuda Triangle	95p ☐

Robert Chapman

Unidentified Flying Objects	95p ☐

Robin Collyns

Did Spacemen Colonise the Earth?	75p ☐

Rupert Furneaux

The Tungus Event	60p ☐

Adi-Kent Thomas Jeffrey

Terror Zones	75p ☐

John A Keel

The Cosmic Question	75p ☐

All these books are available at your local bookshop or newsagent, or can be ordered direct from the publisher. Just tick the titles you want and fill in the form below.

Name ....

Address ....

....

Write to Panther Cash Sales, PO Box 11, Falmouth, Cornwall TR10 9EN.

Please enclose remittance to the value of the cover price plus:

UK: 25p for the first book plus 10p per copy for each additional book ordered to a maximum charge of £1.05.

BFPO and EIRE: 25p for the first book plus 10p per copy for the next 8 books, thereafter 5p per book.

OVERSEAS: 40p for the first book and 12p for each additional book.
Granada Publishing reserve the right to show new retail prices on covers, which may differ from those previously advertised in the text or elsewhere.